Babe

IOWA STATE UNIVERSITY PRESS / AMES

Babe

AN IOWA LEGEND

by *Chuck Offenburger*

with a Foreword by *E. Wayne Cooley*

The photograph on page 12 is from Wide World Photos, Inc., reprinted by permission. The photographs on pages 95, 96, and 153 are from the *Des Moines Register*, reprinted by permission. All the other photographs are from the collection of Babe Bisignano.

The collected tapes of the interviews for this book are available from the Des Moines Public Library.

© 1989 Iowa State University Press, Ames, Iowa 50010

Manufactured in the United States of America

First edition, 1989

Library of Congress Cataloging-in-Publication Data

Offenburger, Chuck.
    Babe Bisignano : an Iowa legend / by Chuck Offenburger : with a foreword by E. Wayne Cooley. — 1st ed.
       p.   cm.
    ISBN 0-8138-0269-5
    ISBN 0-8138-0268-7 (pbk.)
    1. Bisignano, Babe. 2. Restaurateurs—Iowa—Biography.
I. Title.
TX910.5.B57034   1989
647'.95'0924—dc19
[B]   88-37461
                                             CIP

CONTENTS

FOREWORD by E. Wayne Cooley

I HAVE LONG BEEN CONVINCED that the life story of my friend Babe Bisignano is a piece of Iowa lore that should be told in book form— and yes, part of the convincing was done by Babe himself.

For thirty-five years, I have been executive secretary of the Iowa Girls' High School Athletic Union, which is based in Des Moines, and for twenty-seven of those years, I have been dealing with Babe. First, it was just a business relationship. The Union sponsors and fosters sports competition for high school girls from across the state, and as a result we have become a substantial business. We have meetings that go on for hours, and our people often eat out before heading for home. In the years when our offices were in downtown Des Moines, we wound up going to Babe's restaurant more often than any other. He appreciated the business, and we appreciated his hospitality and his personal attention—so much so that we still go there all these many years later.

He's told people that I am his best customer, both from business from the high school tournament crowds and also from personal business my wife and I give him. We eat there often. Out of all that, a friendship has grown to the point where now it's an unusual day that the two of us don't speak on the phone at least once.

I have long enjoyed him, and I've also been fascinated by him, for I know when I'm dealing with him, either as a friend or as a business associate, I'm dealing with—as Iowa State coach Johnny Orr says in this book—a "character the likes of which we will not see again."

Without a doubt, it can be said that Babe Bisignano is one of the best-known men in the state of Iowa. It's my personal view that he is THE best known. Everybody knows him! And it extends beyond Iowa, probably because of all those World War II years when military people from everywhere were hanging out at his tavern and restaurant when they were in Des Moines.

Everybody has their favorite "Babe story," and I do, too. Mine goes back to a trip I took with him and two other guys in the mid-1950s. At the time, I was a stockholder in the Chicago Cubs baseball team, and for several years the four of us had a tradition of making a weekend trip into Chicago for games, where we'd take turns being the host, maker of all arrangements, and payer of all bills.

Well, the year came when it was Babe's turn. By then, the three of us were well aware of what an ego he has. So we flew to Chicago and got a taxi to our hotel. When we got out of the cab, the doorman immediately said, "Mr. Babe, good to see you again!" We went into the lobby, and the bellman came over to get our luggage and he said, "Babe, glad to have you back!" Right then, a vice-president of this hotel who had his desk in the lobby jumped up, ran over, and personally greeted him. The other three of us were starting to be impressed.

Then we went out to Wrigley Field, and the cab driver on the way knew him. We got to the stadium gate, and the ticket taker said, "Mr. Babe, I've been expecting you!" We were really impressed. Babe turned around to us and said, "See, everybody knows me—EVERYBODY!"

We started for our seats, which were behind the third base dugout. We were walking down through the grandstand, and somebody in the crowd yelled at him. We would have really been amazed at that, except that this guy in the crowd yelled, "Hey, Babe! How long you been outta the pen?"

The other three of us broke up laughing, but Babe was furious. He turned right around and marched out of that ball park, and we didn't see him again until we got back to the hotel after the game. He was asleep on the bed. Of course, we never let him forget how well everybody remembers him.

Over the years, I have seen him at his best and at his worst. At his best, he is one of the most compassionate men I've ever known. He has this great well of loving and caring. He'll do anything to help people, and a lot of them are people who get turned away by others.

At his worst, he has a hard-headedness and arrogance that invites trouble, but that's a facade. The man is a pussycat! I don't know another man who is so quick to cry—actual tears—at someone's misfortune. And the truth is, I think he's mellowed a lot over the last five or six years as he's felt age come on. I think God has been talking to him, and that's made him a more pleasant person.

He is a really complex man. There are things here that will make you cheer and that will make you wince. I always thought that any book about him, if ever written, would turn out that way. Babe has been telling me for years that he wanted to get one done. He tried to hire other people to write it, and he tried to write it himself.

In the middle of June 1988, I was host in my office for a meeting between Babe and Chuck Offenburger. The subject was Offenburger's proposal to do the book that Babe had talked about for so long. Babe wanted the author to run the whole proposal by me so that I could give an opinion on it—he often asks me for advice.

I look on Offenburger, with whom I've dealt for years, as a talented journalist with keen insight into what makes people tick. That's why, after listening to both of them, I recommended that they proceed. They did. And the result of their work is now here in print, with all of Babe's glory, warts, and pain.

I keep going back to what Johnny Orr said—we won't see the likes of Babe Bisignano again. It's high time the story was told, and I'm happy I played a role in making it happen.

Des Moines, Iowa
December 1988

Babe

1

THE LEGENDARY CHARACTER

"But make it sound

ike I've got humility."

AS WITH SO MANY of my published tales, for me the Babe Bisignano story began in my old hometown of Shenandoah, Iowa. It was 1958, possibly 1959, and I was eleven or twelve years old.

The priest at St. Mary's Catholic Church was one Msgr. Paul Marasco, native of Des Moines, the first Italian I ever remember meeting. I quickly came to understand Italian anger, contrariness, stubbornness, passion, self-pity, and ultimate goodness, for I was one of the monsignor's altar boys at the time.

What happened on that autumn day, I've come to understand as an adult, was that Monsignor Marasco had earlier asked whatever form of a parish council that existed at that time to purchase a new organ for the church. Being small town Iowans and knowing that the old organ still seemed to be working, they said no. Whereupon, he went around them.

Unbeknownst to me, and I guess unbeknownst to anyone else in the parish, he called an old friend in Des Moines, his boyhood pal Babe Bisignano. This man Bisignano bought a new organ and ordered it delivered and installed in the Shenandoah church. Well, there came a Sunday when the work was all done. Morning Mass was held as usual, with no announcement of special events that afternoon. But late that morning, my mother Anna received a phone call from the rectory telling her to have "Chuckie" at the church by 1:45 P.M. to serve a two o'clock Mass.

Little "Chuckie," as you can imagine, was at the church in full cassock and surplus at the appointed time, not having a clue as to what was happening. And what was that? It was a special, invitation-only dedication Mass for the new organ, and no one from the home church had an invitation. Carrying the tall crucifix on a stick and in the tow of the fully robed monsignor, I stood outside the front of the church, waiting— for what I didn't know.

Suddenly, around the Thomas Avenue corner came a line of the biggest, bluest, and blackest Cadillacs I'd ever seen. They stopped immediately in front of the church, just the way I'd seen escorted funeral processions do. And out of the first Cadillac jumped a formally dressed man, the most striking-looking man I'd ever seen. And he seemed to have lots of men-lieutenants and secretaries—or at least snazzy women— with him. He sure didn't look like anybody from Shenandoah, I knew that.

The twelve-year-old altar boy reasonably concluded that this man was surely either (1) the PRESIDENT, (2) the POPE, or (3) at least somebody who was VERY IMPORTANT. The man embraced Monsignor Marasco. Sloppy cheek kisses, all that. And then we went through a sort of procession into the church, then the Mass, then a private reception afterward.

It was only later that I learned I had had my first look at Alphonse "Babe" Bisignano. And it was a whole lot later— I'm talking years—when I learned I had had an early brush with an Iowa legend.

I grew up and came to His Town, Des Moines, to become a reporter and eventually a columnist for the *Des Moines Register*. He was still Babe Bisignano, still a restaurateur, to be sure, but so much, much more than just that. The altar boy, now an adult, could recognize Bisignano as an elegant character, often outrageous, the likes of which will not be seen again in our time. A source of great stories, great tips, great fun, and sometimes great frustration.

This is a man who

—As a boy, saw his mother get "busted" for bootlegging and then went through it himself later, too.

—Spent ten years in the ring boxing and wrestling, an experience he is alternately proud of and not proud of, as when he said, "What the hell, when you do that, you're really nothing more than an animal."

—Introduced the pizza to Iowa.

—Once "fixed" a dog show.

—Says the Rosary every day.

—Has bet on golf games he's been involved in to the tune of $4,000 per hole.

—Swears he's never had anything to do with the Mafia and yet tells how he and a self-reputed Mafioso named Luigi Fratto once bent a would-be union organizer over a window-sill eight stories up in the Savery Hotel and thus persuaded him to leave Bisignano's operation alone.

—Horrified a prim and proper Columbus Day banquet audience of several hundred people in Des Moines when he introduced Richard Turner, then the attorney general of Iowa, as "the greatest son of a bitch I've ever known."

—Has given away more than a hundred thousand dollars to panhandlers who approach him on the street.

—Describes most newspaper people as "just another typical newspaper prick."

—Could get away with walking up to a presidential candidate, as he did Alexander Haig in late 1987, and say, "You know, the reason I like you is because you got balls." (For the record, Haig's response during that reception at Babe's restaurant was, "Well, thank you, Babe, but the truth is a lot of people have taken swipes at 'em, too.")

—Counts as his closest friends a number of the biggest hoods and greatest nuns the city of Des Moines has ever known.

—Is now observing his fiftieth year in business in downtown Des Moines and has recently opened a new joint on the north side, too.

Needless to say, Bisignano quickly became almost a fixture in my *Register* column, appearing with more regularity than any other Iowan over a decade. And he was always so willing to say why he was there: "If you don't have me in your column at least every three weeks, people will quit reading you. But make it sound like I've got humility."

And so the stories flowed in the column.

We also became friends, even though at this writing he is seventy-five years old and I'm forty-one. And as I became better known in Iowa—certainly not better known than Bisignano but well known just the same—the two of us often wound up as traveling partners for benefit golf dinners and other events for which the public wanted not just one clown, but two.

That gave me a chance for a firsthand look at the quintessential Babe Bisignano. I will never forget a trip to Clarinda in southwest Iowa in the spring of 1988. I had an earlier speeding ticket, which required a stop in Corning during our trip. I had no money, which is my usual state, so I borrowed a hundred dollars from him when we stopped in midafternoon at the Adams County Courthouse. He said that while I went in and settled with Justice, he would meander downtown in Corning and see what was happening.

I paid the ticket, then drove downtown in Corning to find him. There he was, standing quizzically in front of a storefront that had on its overhead sign "Connie's Salon."

"Hey," he said when I asked him what he was doing,

6

"what do you make of this joint? I saw that 'Salon' up there and I decided to go in and have a little drink. You know what? There were a bunch of broads in there getting their hair cut! It's a damned beauty parlor, that's what it is!"

This is a man who has done up to, maybe more than, two million dollars in business in a year's time. He employs nearly one hundred people and has for fifty years. He has access to the nation's great and powerful and famous. A success if ever there was one. And here he is standing on the main drag of Corning, Iowa, stymied by simple spelling. I knew about his eighth-grade semieducation and his notorious lack of attention to the academic refinements of American life. But still.

He ultimately convinced me of his honest befuddlement, so I took time and explained the difference between a "salon" and a "saloon." Then we visited one of the latter.

It was there, and on the rest of that trip, that he told me of his desire to get a book written about his life and his frustrations in trying to do so. He'd tried to do it himself—you ought to see the manuscript of a man who doesn't understand the difference between a salon and a saloon. Uh, on second thought, you shouldn't.

As long ago as 1947, the year I was born, he had hired a writer named Duncan Underhill, a former reporter for the *New York Times* and other papers and then a Hollywood screenwriter, to come live above the Bisignano garage in Des Moines and write the Great Book, which might have been a bit premature had it ever really happened, given the fact that Babe had only been in business for eight years and that his celebrity in the state then was only a fraction of what it is today.

Underhill went to work and in a November 1947 interview with the *Des Moines Tribune* said: "The book begins with the first night Bisignano went to the Polk County jail to begin serving a six-month term for contempt of court," which actually happened, as you will discover here. "From this point, the book reverts to the life of Bisignano, following it through his school days, his days as a shoe shine boy, his boxing and wrestling career and his nightclub business." Of course, a lot of that is going to happen in this book, too.

But there's a difference, or a couple of differences. One is that Duncan Underhill said his book, which he intended to fictionalize, would "end with Bisignano being a prosperous farmer." I was dumbfounded when I came across that clipping. Bisignano is a man who, late in his life, has told me that one of his goals is to "buy a pair of blue jeans because I haven't had on a pair since I was a boy." Prosperous farmer, indeed.

Another difference is that Bisignano wound up getting mad at Underhill and firing him as his book writer—and I guess this is a good place to point out that Bisignano has neither a financial interest in nor control over the effort you are reading now.

But it's also important that Bisignano fired that writer for what seem to be wholly justifiable reasons. "Duncan was a great guy, and he'd come in from the garage and help my wife with the housework and tell our kids stories and all that," Babe recalled. "But he also drank so much I couldn't believe it. He'd get so drunk, we'd have to get a ladder out and crawl up to one of the windows on the garage apartment to see if he was still alive.

"Well, one day, I'm down at the restaurant downtown and I get this call from a guy out at the Greenwood Tavern, and he tells me I better get out there right away. I ask what's going on, and he says, 'That crazy Duncan is down here with your dog, Mr. Bisignano, and he's trying to trade the dog in for a six-pack of beer.' That was the end of Duncan."

*A*lphonse James "Babe" Bisignano has always had a nose for being where news is made. His persona and his antics have attracted the attention of Des Moines Register cartoonists Frank Miller and, in later years, Brian Duffy. And in addition, photographers have often captured Babe being the character that he is. For example, there was the time in the early 1980s when Elaine Szymoniak, a well-known Des Moines politician, and several other pro-Choice advocates picketed his restaurant because a Right-to-Life group was having a meeting there. Babe's reaction to the picket line was to picket the pickets. Earlier, in 1961, when he thought the Drake University Bulldog basketball team should have been invited to participate in the National Invitational Tournament in New York City's Madison Square Garden, he had no qualms about going to the Garden to picket. And in 1972, when the movie The Godfather was all the rage, he represented the feelings of a lot of Italian-Americans when he took to the streets in front of a Des Moines theater to protest the film.

Babe, as drawn by Frank Miller.

Brian Duffy's look at a legend.

Picketing a picketer, Elaine Szymoniak.

Picketing for the Bulldogs.

Picketing for Italians.

The ultimate outcome of that is that the Babe Bisignano story has gone untold, despite some more recent feeble efforts by Babe himself to put pen to paper, until now. I walked into the restaurant in June of 1988 and said, "On that book you've been talking about for so long, this is put up or shut up time. I want to do it."

He agreed. He put up. And he put up with a lot—some twenty hours of interviews, searches of his files for photographs and lots of other inconveniences. It was a process that confirmed in my own mind the worthiness of his story and, until late in the process, confirmed a friendship.

Jim Flansburg, a veteran *Des Moines Register* reporter and Babe-watcher and now the editor of the editorial pages, at one point angered Bisignano by telling him, "Before this is over, you and Offenburger will be at each other's throat." Bisignano said it would never happen. We went on with our chats, and for a long time we seemed as tight personally as ever.

It is a relationship, old dog and medium-age dog, that has amazed even his children. His oldest son, Joe, now fifty-two, told me, "In a lot of ways, I've seen you and Dad having the kind of relationship he thinks he should have with his sons."

And at one point during our interviews, when I was asking Babe to make quick quips and comments about a number of his well-known friends and enemies in Iowa, I raised my own name. "Chuck Offenburger?" he said. "Like my son."

He even named his restaurant's biggest-selling sandwich (a glorified hamburger) after me, doing so without checking with me or the *Register* first. Some of the bosses got hot, but mostly they just joined me in smiling about it. "The Offenburger," the menus say, "Iowa Boy's favorite. Ground Chuck, ham, melted Swiss, lettuce, and tomato."

Alas, Flansburg was right. For before Bisignano and I

were finished, we did wind up at each other's throat—all over an issue of what would be contained in this book. What's here, I assure you, is what I think ought to be here for the story to be truly told, and in some cases it is definitely not what he thinks should be here.

Tough, I told him, when he objected. And that's when he screamed in a boozy late night phone call that he was all through putting up and thereafter would shut up, which, of course, Babe Bisignano will never do in a general sense even if he does so around me.

Alas, Joe Bisignano was also right. Babe's pique with me at the end makes me a lot like his sons and his daughter. He's mad at them, too, as you'll discover, and has been for years. That's sad. But he is still a story—and a character—the likes of which we will never again see in Iowa. Why?

Johnny Orr, the Iowa State University basketball coach and a great friend of Bisignano, probably answered that best. "The things Babe has done in his past—and I mean they're some wild things, coach—well, nobody could do that today and still be respected," Orr said. "He did them in a time when that kind of stuff just meant you were a character. It couldn't happen again today."

So here we go with the Babe Bisignano story.

"I've been trying to get this done since 1947," he said at the top of our very first interview. "And I want to tell you that now that it's finally happening, I'm more nervous than I was before my first boxing match."

Put yourself in the role of the referee and read on.

2

BECOMING "BABE,"
FOREVERMORE AN ACTOR

"I'm on stage

very night . . ."

IN A GREAT BIT OF CASTING in 1958, the Des Moines Community Playhouse directors asked Babe Bisignano to play the slickly dressed, rough-talking gambler "Big Jule" in a production of *Guys and Dolls*, a delightful musical based on the stories and characters of the old-time New York newspaperman Damon Runyon. If ever there was a Damon Runyon character, Babe Bisignano is one.

"We'd work through the noon hour rush at the restaurant," said Fred Eckrosh, a great Bisignano friend and for thirty years an employee. "Then we'd go get in the car. I'd drive and Babe would study his lines for that play and recite them. You can imagine him trying to learn lines. We'd spend hours out there, driving all over Polk County. Actually, he did pretty well, though. He memorized about half of what he was supposed to, and the rest he just made up. But they packed them in for that play, they had to hold it over, and I think a lot of it was just because of him.

"You've got to remember, there's more ham in that guy than there is in a hog."

Playing the part turned out to be no big deal, Bisignano

17

says now, even though he'd never done anything like that. "After all," he said, "I'm on stage every night and have been for fifty years."

He was referring to his work at his restaurants. His is a unique role in restaurant operation. "Look, I don't know how to cook an egg or mix a drink, but I'll tell you what, I've got the ability to try some dish or try some drink and know whether it's done right. And put me out in the dining room, I'm the best 'front' man there is. Nobody knows how to work the public better than me. And when people come in, they know that sooner or later, I'm going to drop by their table and talk to them, buy them a drink, whatever. If they've got their little kids with them, I make all over them, even if they're ugly.

"And I'm always running around with a towel and cleaning up the table and carrying the dishes away. That's why I got that nickname as the 'millionaire busboy.'"

What has really sold the public on his place downtown, and what will probably ultimately sell them on a new, smaller restaurant he opened in the last year on the northwest side of Des Moines, is the persona of Babe Bisignano, his Damon Runyon-ness. He is a cat cut in another time—a little rough, a little naughty and yet totally personable most of the time.

The stories roll out of him for the customers at a mile a minute, perhaps sometimes exaggerated, but usually funny and always intriguing. Sometimes when he gets to telling them, his backhands to the listeners' shoulders—he does that for emphasis—get a little rough but most tolerate them.

"Yeah, I'm on stage every night," he repeats.

So, when did the show start?

You might take it from World War II when his business boomed with the influx of Women's Army Corps trainees. Fifteen thousand of them were at Fort Des Moines, and most

of them hung out at Babe's when they were off duty, naturally drawing in every young guy who was still around the
territory. I'll talk some more about that later.

You might take it all the way back to his childhood. God,
it was rugged, especially if judged against today's norms of
growing up. He had to live by his fists and his wits, selling
newspapers, shining shoes, hustling grips for railroad trav-
elers, running booze—whatever it took.

But most likely you'd start the show on a morning in
1929 when a sixteen-year-old Alphonse Bisignano walked
into the office of boxing promoter Paul Louis "Pinkie" George
in the old Des Moines Coliseum and asked him if he could get
a spot on a fight card that Pinkie was putting together.

"What's your name?" George, eighty-three years old at
this writing, asked him.

"Alphonse Bisignano."

"Are you Italian?"

"Of course."

"That name is too long," the promoter said. "There's an
Italian boxing champ named Primo Carnera. How about if we
call you 'Baby Carnera'?"

"Call me anything you want to if you'll give me a place
on that card," the youngster said.

It was innocent hype that went toward still-innocent
public fraud a few short years later when he switched from
boxing to wrestling, or "rasslin'." He recalls a promoter in
New York City heralding his arrival in town to the media as
being the coming of the next great Italian champion. "They
took me down to the pier and had me all dressed up as an
Italian immigrant, with this little cap on and carrying a tat-
tered suitcase," he said. "They snuck me up on a boat called
the *Europa* and then had me walk down the gangplank like I
just got here. It was the first time I'd ever been on a ship like
that. But the photographers loved it. After the papers came
out, I'd go into Italian joints there in New York, and I mean, I
couldn't buy a drink. Everybody was falling all over me."

The "Baby" was later shortened to "Babe," and he eventually resumed using the last name of Bisignano instead of Carnera. But I'll argue that it was precisely at that moment with Pinkie George in the Des Moines Coliseum office that the Babe show began. For it was then that Alphonse became, uh . . . well . . . you could argue that it was then that he became something he was not, or you could put a nicer gloss on it and say it was then that he became something more than what he really was.

I like the latter because I think the truth is that Babe Bisignano has spent sixty years since then being essentially larger than life in a lot of people's minds. He's come to understand during this long-running performance the special agony that a lot of larger-than-life actors go through when they mask their own emotions—especially after the 1979 death of his wife, Catherine, from cancer.

"People read all about me doing this and doing that, fun stuff, and they see me down there at the restaurants being a Good Time Joe and all happy and everything," he said in his seventy-fifth year. "I know everybody and everybody is my friend. The truth is, man, I'm the loneliest son of a bitch in town."

How did it get this way?

3

WHERE HE CAME FROM

"[The beatings] would scare the hell out of all of us kids."

FOR ALPHONSE JAMES BISIGNANO, born March 14, 1913, in Des Moines, and for his three brothers and two sisters, it was a horrible childhood. There's no way else to put it, although Babe himself won't say it that strongly.

"No point in being bitter about it now," he said. "I never really had a good father, the way most people do. I had a good mother, but not for long. Yeah, it was real hard, but if I hadn't had that kind of childhood, I wouldn't have made it as far as I have."

They lived in "Little Italy" on Des Moines' south side, and life was tough. It was even tougher on them than it was on everybody else in Little Italy in what was a tough, tough time. Mother Lena, the anchor of the family and a native of Naples, Italy, was by all descriptions a saint of a woman who died at the age of thirty-five in 1923, when Babe was ten.

First Communion.

*I*t is almost hard to believe that the innocent, angelic-looking little boy in the First Communion picture grew up to do all that Babe Bisignano has done. His parents, Genaro and Lena, are shown in their wedding picture, and there is an undated photo of Genaro's mother, Mary, who was the grandmother who essentially raised the children after Lena died and Genaro fled. Speaking about the growing-up period, brother Chuck said, "There was no psychology back then, no counseling. The way my father was was the way he knew, and it wasn't much different for us than it was for a lot of kids. The iron hand ruled. If you didn't follow the rules, you got the hell beat out of you. Then, it was considered discipline. By today's standards, it might well be considered child abuse." Despite how unsettling the growing-up process was, the young Babe Bisignano, as seen in a 1930 photograph, turned into a handsome young man.

Babe's parents, Lena and Genaro.

Babe's grandmother, Mary.

Babe, his brothers, and his sisters.

The 1930 Babe.

Neither Babe nor any of his siblings are sure what she died of, except they remember it was during an operation in a hospital and they all suspect it was liver-related.

Their father Genaro, or George as he was called after he came to the United States from Terravecchia, Italy, was by today's standards a schnook of a dad who, five years after his wife's death, just flat abandoned the five children who were still living. He was leaving for Chicago to "find work," he told them, and he would "send money."

Send money? "He didn't even send a postcard—never, ever!" Babe said. "We heard nothing at all of him for thirty years, and then it was bad. He finally came back to Des Moines when he was an old, old man, and when he did, he embarrassed the hell out of all of us."

But we'll get to that bad reunion scene later. For now, the best characterization of Genaro Bisignano comes from Babe's little sis, Felicia Kelleher, now seventy-one, called "Dee" by everyone. "Mother's Day has always been hard for me to face, even to this day, for Momma having died so young," she said in a session in her Des Moines home. "But I've said, too, that God knew what He was doing taking her in her thirties so that she didn't have to live with that bastard for a longer life."

But let's get the family sorted out. From Genaro, who died in 1961, and Lena came the following children:

—Mary, the oldest, who died in 1964 after having grown up fighting the South Side ruffians who were picking on her little brother, Alphonse, and who ultimately wound up in a restaurant business in Des Moines, and in doing so really angered him.

—Alphonse, or Babe.

—Felicia, or Dee, whom you met above. Retired now, she

also worked in restaurants, as well as for the state government and for Younkers department store.

—Chuck, now seventy, who has his own successful restaurant in the Highland Park neighborhood on the north side of Des Moines. He neither looks nor acts like Babe. "He's been in the limelight, and I haven't, and I respect that," Chuck said. "I don't want to be. That's his life. I'm happy with my life. Sure, he pisses me off sometimes, especially about his kids, but I hope he lives to a ripe old age. Whatever it is, it will be interesting. It always has been with Babe."

—Jimmy, who died in infancy a year after his mother's death.

—Frankie, who died in 1985 and who had earlier meandered from Des Moines to California for a time, ultimately returning to help his sister Mary run the restaurant that so angered their brother Alphonse. (To understand the impact of their venture on Babe, you should also know that their place, located only a block away from his newly successful operation downtown, was called "Bambino's.")

Another very important person in those early years was grandmother Mary Bisignano, who for a time took the Bisignano kids after her son Genaro abandoned his family. She did the best she could, even though as Babe remembers, "The only words she knew in English were 'Go to hell!' "

Knowing English was one of the advantages that Lena Bisignano had over other Italian women in the neighborhood in Babe's earliest years. "They were all making home-brewed beer and wine," he said, "but my mother was one of the best. And because she knew English, she would interpret for a lot of the other women down there. I can't remember that either my mother or my father ever drank themselves, but here she was making it. And she'd fix meals for people who would come into our home and eat them. It was never a real restaurant operation, but she did a good business. Most of the customers were Irish and Jewish people from around there. As a result, she always had some money and we dressed a whole lot better than most of the kids in the neighborhood did.

"She'd get grapes by the ton from California to make the wine, and we'd have to stomp them. Since I was sort of a fat, chubby kid, I was always a pretty good stomper."

The mother's business and financial success was in marked contrast to that of her husband, Genaro. "Before he left, he was a guy who chased rainbows," Babe said. "He was always dressed well, suits and ties and silk shirts that my mother would get ready for him. He always had a pocketful of fountain pens, and he always carried one of those leather grips like lawyers carry—you know, a briefcase sort of deal.

"He sold some insurance, and at one time he ran some sort of coal company, but it seemed like he'd always come back to cooking at some little bar or cafe." Nonetheless, he ruled at home, with an especially firm hand.

"We started out on Granger Avenue, but my mother was always one to go for improvement, and eventually we moved over to Courtland Avenue," Babe said. "My mother was so good that most of her customers followed her to buy her wine and beer or for her meals. I can remember when I was about nine years old, I came home from school one day. The heat must have been on, because there was the county sheriff and he was opening up my mom's kegs and pouring them down the drain. She got raided, that's what it really was.

"My dad was a guy that never wanted my mother's customers around when he came home, even though she was the one who was making all the money that let us get by. He came home that day and found out about the raid, and he raised hell. He told her if she hadn't wanted to move out of the old neighborhood, this would never have happened.

"He used to beat her up, and I think he did that night. It would scare the hell out of all of us kids, and we'd go hide under the beds. Looking back on it, if I'd been a little bit bigger, I would have taken a ball bat to him. I'd have killed him for that."

Brother Chuck remembers it about the same way, although being younger he naturally focuses on how it was for the kids instead of how it was for his mother.

"There was no psychology back then, no counseling," he said. "The way my father was was the way he knew, and it wasn't much different for us than it was for a lot of kids. The iron hand ruled. If you didn't follow the rules, you got the hell beat out of you. Then, it was considered discipline. By today's standards, it might well be considered child abuse."

4

GROWING UP FAST

". . . I got kicked out o

hree schools in one day."

RALPH COSTANZO is a retired Des Moines businessman, now seventy-five years old. He grew up in Little Italy, too, and he's known Alphonse Bisignano, boy and man. He's so close, in fact, that even now he calls Babe every morning at six-thirty.

"I'm checking to see if he's still alive and all right," Costanzo said. "If he doesn't answer the phone, I start calling the funeral homes."

So what was Bisignano really like as a youngster in those years on the South Side? "Good guy, big for his age and pretty tough when he needed to be," Costanzo said. "I'll never forget one time, though, when we were playing ball or something, and he wound up beating me up all the way home. When we get there, my mother socked him with a tree limb."

Carl Cacciatore, a few years younger, was still in the same crowd. "Being a little guy, when the other kids would pick on me, Babe often would go after them," he said.

They both can remember Bisignano in his earliest times. "We were all poor," Cacciatore said. "One of our duties as kids was to go hop on a coal train as it was passing and throw off chunks of coal. Then we'd go back with burlap bags, pick up the coal, and take it home so we could have some heat."

They can remember Lena Bisignano passing away, Genaro Bisignano leaving, and the family foundering, despite the best efforts of Grandmother Mary Bisignano, who took charge as best she could. All of Little Italy was shocked, both said, especially when it became clear the father was not coming back.

They saw Alphonse go to work selling newspapers—up at five A.M. and on his corner at Sixth Avenue and Mulberry Street, protecting his corner against bullies who wanted to butt in on his business, which was purchasing the papers for one cent and selling them for two on the busiest corner he could find and defend. He'd repeat the operation later every day when the afternoon papers came out. In early adolescence, they saw him shine shoes at barber shops.

They saw him as an athlete. "He was always a pitcher when we were little kids," Costanzo said. "He threw that ball so hard you wouldn't believe it, but he didn't know where it was going and neither did anybody else."

And they remember his "education," as does his sister, Dee Kelleher. "When Babe started to get bigger, what he was always getting into trouble for was fighting," she said. "In some ways, maybe he was a bully, but in others, he was going back to some of those bigger kids who'd given him trouble when he was littler. He still had a big heart, just like he does now, but fighting was his problem at every school he went to."

Uh, every school he went to? How many was that? "I must have set some kind of record because I got kicked out of three schools in one day," the man himself confessed. "It started at St. Anthony's School, which is the one that I always seemed to wind up going back to, too. But those nuns were tough, and they had their pets, even back then. The only one who ever seemed to like me was Sister Mary

Clothilda. She was kind of a rough-looking, rough-talking old soul, a lot like me. I got along okay with her, but the rest of them I had trouble with.

"I didn't do good in school. It wasn't that I was stupid, but I didn't like school all that much. Maybe you'd say I was kind of a sleepy kid, but remember I was getting up at five every morning to go sell papers. My mind was always more on making a buck.

"So one day, I suppose I was about thirteen, I got thrown out of St. Anthony's for fighting. I got sent to Father [Cornelius] Lally. He was good to me—he'd have me out of class half the time doing janitor work anyway—but this time he just had to get me out of there because I'd been fighting. So he called down to St. John's School and told them he was sending me. I went in there with kind of a black mark against me.

"By now, we're at about recess time in the middle of the morning. They told me they had this bell system, and the different number of bells meant different things. But they said if it was more than three bells, it meant a fire. So I'm there and the bells started ringing. I waited and three of them rang. I got nervous and started hollering 'Fire! Fire!' and I had all of those kids running out on to the playground. The problem was, they were signaling something else. I always say since then that I was one bell away from being a hero, but instead, I got expelled.

"So I went back to St. Anthony's, and it's about noon. Father Lally called St. Mary's School, and after the nuns there heard what had happened, *they* wouldn't even take me. So there was the three schools in one day. I wound up going to Washington Public School for a while.

"The main difference between public school and Catholic school," he continued, "was that the teachers in the public school couldn't take a rubber hose to you and they couldn't use a ruler to whack you across the knuckles. But I wound up eighth grade at St. Ambrose School. And that's where I got expelled again, but, hey, this has got to be even more of a record—they kicked me out after school was all over! Can you imagine that? I'd done all the work and finished, but they refused to give me a diploma."

Why?

"For kissing Rosie Fusaro," he said. "She was in my class and she was my girlfriend. After that last day of school, we were told to get back there later on for rehearsal for graduation. So Rosie and I are walking home through this little park, and I backed her up against a big tree and gave her a little kiss. What I didn't know was that this old woman across the street saw me do it, and she called the school.

"When I got back there for rehearsal, this nun told me I wouldn't be graduating. I said, 'Why?' She said, 'For kissing Rosie Fusaro in the park.' I said, 'Well, is Rosie graduating?' She said, 'Yes, because I know you led her on.' Can you imagine a bum rap like that? So I never graduated."

Rosie Fusaro Stilwell, now seventy-five and living in Covina, California, confirmed this story, "except that I don't remember no tree." Well, was he a good kisser? "I already told you I enjoyed it, didn't I?" she said. "And maybe you'll want to write this down. My brother Patrick died in Des Moines in November of 1987. I was back for the funeral, and Babe was there, too. For the record, I got another kiss then."

Even though he had kissed off his eighth-grade diploma, Alphonse was admitted to the Des Moines Catholic Academy, which is now Dowling High School, the next fall for what he says was one basic reason: "I was big, and they wanted me to play football.

"I was good enough and rough enough that I played that one year as a left tackle. I never could understand the plays in the huddle, but this guy Gaspar Sarcone would explain them to me in Italian while we were running up to the line.

"Then basketball season came, and I went out, but I was the worst. Every time I'd shoot the ball, it would hit that backboard so hard it would come bouncing way, way off of there. So instead of having me play, what they'd do is to have

34

me box somebody at halftime as a way of drawing a crowd to the game. It was crazy."

Baseball season came. Bisignano played one game, in right field, and "hit three homers," he said in a boast that would make a truth-seeking baseball fan wonder. But, what the heck, it was a long time ago and what does it matter now?

What happened next was no source of wonder but rather was pitiful: Genaro Bisignano left Des Moines and his children. Alphonse's semieducation was over. He entered the School of Hard Knocks—that's hard knocks both in boxing and in a rough life—and he was forever changed.

"Grandma took charge as best she could," he recalled. "I was doing everything I could to bring home some money for food, and so was my older sister Mary. But finally, I guess some of the neighbors told the juvenile court people and we all wound up in Judge Myers's court.

"Mary and Felicia (Dee) went to the Sisters of Humility at their place in Ottumwa. I was given permission to quit school and go to work. They sent Chuck to Father Flanagan's Boys Home for a while. Frankie was the littlest, and he stayed with Grandma."

Alphonse snared a job as a "go-fer" at the Des Moines Golf and Country Club, living in the locker-room. "That sounds bad, but it was good," he said. "I'd caddy some, run errands during the poker games, and go get the alcohol that the guys were using to spike their 'near beer.' It was good because, living there, I was eating New York strip steaks for breakfast. I'd go out and run the golf course and stay in shape. But then I got busted for the first time.

"I think I was sixteen. One of those times, somebody caught me bringing in that alcohol, and somebody else made a big deal out of it. The manager of the club, even though he knew all about it, said he just couldn't have that going on,

35

and he fired me. I moved into the Plaza Hotel downtown. I was still just a kid. But I started hustling booze, getting it in four-ounce and eight-ounce containers and delivering it to wherever it'd been ordered."

He also worked for a time as a "shill" in a local craps game—in other words, available when someone was looking for a game and sometimes losing on purpose to lure them further into the action. It was then that he started having some income, and it was also then that he started meeting some truly shifty characters, like the two guys who came into the gambling house one night and said they had a bunch of women's clothing to sell at cheap prices.

"I was thinking of my two sisters down there at the convent in Ottumwa and how they probably needed some clothes, so I bought them four dresses from these two guys and sent the dresses down to them," Babe said. "I got the nicest letter back from my sister Mary, thanking me for the dresses and saying how thoughtful that was. But about two weeks later, I was there at the gambling joint and in comes a detective with those two guys I'd bought the dresses from. They were handcuffed together. The detective said they'd admitted to stealing the dresses, and then they started pointing out everybody in the place who'd bought dresses from them. The cops said they wanted all the dresses back. I said to this detective, 'But I can't get them back because I've given them to my sisters in a convent.' He said, 'I don't care if the pope's got them in the Vatican—I want them back!'

"So the next day, I hitchhiked to Ottumwa and visited my sisters. I felt terrible, but I told them I had to have the dresses back because they'd been stolen before I bought them. They gave them back to me, I put them in a sack and late that afternoon I started hitchhiking back to Des Moines. But it got dark before I got very far from Ottumwa, and I knew I was going to have trouble getting another ride. I was standing there beside the road for a long time, and it was getting really dark. I noticed there was a golf course right across the highway, and it had a green right there. So I figured that would be a good place to sleep. I went over there and used the sack with the dreses in it as a pillow. But then in the night I woke up and realized I was cold and getting all wet from the dew. So I took those dresses out and put them on as best I could to stay warm. They were pretty small, so I split them out at the seams and all that. But they did keep me warm.

"That next morning, I took them off, wadded them up in the sack and got a ride on into Des Moines. I went right to the police detective and gave him the dresses, even though they weren't in very good shape by then. I look back on that now and I can say that was the only time anybody ever would've caught Babe Bisignano wearing a dress on a golf course."

In that era, he also held jobs as a car body sander in the old Ford plant in Des Moines, at a meat packing company, and for a time drove a truck delivering dry cleaning and laundry from the Artistic Cleaners, even though when he started he didn't really know how to drive and had no license.

"One of their drivers gave me a lift one day, and I was asking him if he knew where I might get some work," he said. "He told me to go to their office and ask for a guy named Dutch. I did that, and Dutch asked if I could drive. I said yes, even though I couldn't. In fact, the only thing I knew about it was having watched that other guy drive. He asked me if I knew the west side of town and could make deliveries there, and I said yes, even though I didn't have any idea where things were over there. So he gave me a truck and some clothes to deliver and told me to get going.

"I was sitting there in that truck, ready to start, and he was standing right there watching me. I was barely sure of which pedal the clutch was and which one the brake was. I was so nervous I was about to puke. But I said a Hail Mary, pushed a pedal, and hit the starter button. The truck started and somehow I got it out of there. I never bothered to shift out of first gear. It didn't run very smooth that way, but I was moving. It kind of jumped and bumped back to the south side, where I knew I could find some of my friends. One of those guys knew how to drive and he knew the west side pretty well, too, so I talked him into going along and doing the driving the rest of the day. By the end of that day, he'd explained enough about how to drive that I was pretty good after that."

And he started boxing more, first at "smokers," which he said were like "conventions today where the guys might have some girl dancing, but back then, they'd hire us kids to come in and box."

Late in his sixteenth year, already abandoned by his father and busted for selling booze and desperate for money, he went to see Pinkie George in the Coliseum boxing promotion office.

And that's when young Alphonse became Baby Carnera and when a better life began to happen.

5

THE YEARS IN THE RING

"... you've got to be a competitor in life if you want to get anyplace."

PINKIE GEORGE recognized quickly that this rough-cut young Italian boxer he'd renamed Baby Carnera would be a good draw on any fight card . "He's always been what I'd call a freewheeler," George said. "You know, a good actor. He had some pretty good skills when I first saw him, and then when I was promoting him at the Coliseum, I was also bringing in a lot of good fighters from all over everywhere, and Babe got to see a lot of them. They gave him a lot of tips."

At five feet eleven inches and 175 pounds, Babe quickly became light heavyweight boxing champion of Iowa, where he did almost all of his boxing. His coast-to-coast wanderings didn't happen until he switched to wrestling.

He had eighty-seven pro boxing bouts in his three years, winning all but six. "I never got knocked out," he said, "although there were several times I was penalized for being too rough, butting heads and all that."

Rough? He can recall one fight he accepted in Pittsburg, Kansas, that meant his first ride ever in a Pullman railcar. He won it, he recalls, but also remembers being battered enough that "we had to stop in Kansas City on the way home to buy a leech to put on my eye to drain it."

One night at the Coliseum in Des Moines, he broke his hand in an early round. "There was a guy we all called 'Doc' who was a real boxing fan and was always there around the ring," he said. "He came up and said that he noticed I'd hurt my hand. He said if I'd come out to his office, he'd X-ray it, set it, and it wouldn't cost me a dime. So we did that. But when we got to his office and he turned on the lights, you've never heard so much barking. The 'Doc' was a veterinarian! But he still took care of my hand."

Grandma Bisignano, who by then had charge of the family, appreciated the money Babe was bringing home, "but she'd carry on all the time when I'd come home with a bloody towel or something. I'd say, 'Well, Grandma, that isn't my blood—I had to loan my towel to the other boy.' But she'd say, 'Oh! Stop this fighting!' "

His success was a matter of pride among others in the Little Italy neighborhood of Des Moines. "Everybody could remember when he was so poor," said Ralph Costanzo, the boyhood friend, "and they were happy to see him kind of go into the upper bracket some."

After three years, though, Babe, seeing there would never be a whole lot of money in boxing, and growing increasingly fearful of suffering permanent injury, was lured into professional wrestling, in which there was more money, more opportunity for travel, and more opportunity for "a showman like me."

But his first love in the fight game would forever remain boxing. He has served for years as a member of the Iowa State Boxing Commission. "It's a sport that with proper supervision I think should be offered in every school in the state," he said. "It's just you and another guy in a ring. It's a war out there. It's not trying to injure him, and it's not really

40

even trying to hit him. It's trying to not let him hit you. That's why it's called 'the art of self-defense.'

"The best thing it does for you is give you a competitive spirit, and brother, I'll tell you, you've got to be a competitor in life if you want to get anyplace. It's a cold world."

The six-year wrestling career began with Babe "learning my first holds—remember, I didn't know anything about it— in the backseat of a car from a guy named Jack Hader as we were on our way to Lincoln, Nebraska, for our first match. I was a natural, even if I say so myself. I was colorful. I'd play to the crowds, jump over the ropes and all that."

He said the only time he was intimidated in the wrestling ring was "when my opponent either had lots of tattoos or lots of hair all over his back and shoulders."

His real break came when he ran into the Dusek brothers, who were established wrestling stars and pro- moters from Omaha who had come to control most of the wrestling booking in the New York City area. "Rudy Dusek asked me if I wanted to go to New York," Babe said, "and, man, it was like asking me if I wanted to go to the moon. The only question I had about it was that I had a pretty good job working for the City of Des Moines at the time, swinging a pick and shovel on the streets. I went to my boss, who was Paul Halpin, the city engineer, and asked him if I should go to New York. I'll never forget, he said: 'If you're going to be a wrestler, go where the people are. If you're going to stay in Iowa, be a farmer.' "

*I*f there is one thing that has been both the curse and the salvation of Babe Bisignano, it is fighting, both within the ring and outside of it. He's always been a fighter, and he's always admired others who fight. After early days as a boxer—he was light heavyweight champion of Iowa—he went on into wrestling, where his showmanship carried him. His wife, Catherine, willingly joined in the hype, posing for photos in which she was flipping him, and he wrestled such notables as "world champion" Max Baer, who once did an exhibition with him at the Des Moines YMCA. Always portrayed as the Italian—he was called "Baby Carnera" at first after an Italian champion, Primo Carnera—he was also often photographed cooking or eating spaghetti. In 1935 and 1936, two of his biggest years on the national wrestling circuit, he kept careful logs of where he'd wrestled, who his opponents were, and what his take-home pay was. Babe continues to be fascinated with the fight game, as when a bunch of current wrestling stars, Hulk Hogan among them, performed in Des Moines in 1987 and observed one of the wrestlers' birthdays with a dinner at Babe's restaurant. Babe and the Hulk were photographed together, and ever since, Babe has handed out copies of that photo to youngsters, always signing them, "I'm the one on the left."

"Baby Carnera" in his early boxing career.

The wrestler.

Al Bisignano
ITALIAN CHAMPION

Posing with Catherine.

44

Against "world champion" Max Baer.

An "Italian Champion" must like spaghetti, right?

Portions of Babe's 1935 and 1936 wrestling logs.

With a wrestling superstar—Babe on the left.

He indeed went to where the people were—New York mainly but also Toronto, Minneapolis, Los Angeles, and others—and became a star. He got a lot of help from the legendary Earl Wampler, who wrestled as "the coal miner from Scranton, Iowa," and had a following almost worldwide. "Earl went with me on that first trip to New York, and we traveled a lot together and wrestled each other, and he was always good to me," Babe said.

"The only bad thing he ever did to me was one time when we were going to some match somewhere, and we stopped in Oskaloosa on the way so he could stop in and see his daughter, who was a beauty operator there. I stayed in the car, and Earl was in there for a long time. When he came out, he'd had her color his hair. That night, when we were wrestling each other and starting to get all sweated up, that coloring stuff started running out all over his face and all over me. It was awful."

As his trademark holds Bisignano developed the "Italian flip" and the "Italian whip." Generally, he was promoted in the role of the good guy against some dastardly villain—but not always. A long-ago clipping from the Ottumwa, Iowa, *Courier* quoted the local sheriff as saying, "After one or two more wrestling shows our riot squad should be at the peak of efficiency." What he was referring to was a match in which Babe "cuffed his opponent in such a manner as to draw the anger of the customers," resulting in chair and bottle tossing. A return match ended with Babe winning, then picking up his opponent and carrying him "as though he was a baby." The crowd mellowed at first, but then exploded again when Babe dropped the man roughly on the floor of the arena "and near pandemonium broke out."

"Within three months after I started, I was wrestling main events in Minneapolis, and it wasn't long after that, I was doing main events at Madison Square Garden," he said.

He made a lot of money and saw a lot, but he paid for it, too, with "broken ribs, torn knee cartilages, getting my teeth kicked out." One thing "I always dreaded," he said, "was that

49

I might wind up with a cauliflower ear. Some of the young guys wanted them so they'd look rougher, and they'd even hit themselves in the side of the head to get them, but I always was scared about having one."

His wrestling career wound down in late 1938 after an incident at the Olympic Auditorium in Los Angeles, where he'd had a successful run of matches and where he was saluted by the papers as being the "Mussolini Muscle Man from Iowa." He'd become the biggest crowd pleaser on the local cards, especially when he was wrestling a local hero, Vincent Lopez.

"One night before the match, I went to the promoter and I told him I wanted a two-hundred-dollar guarantee, which was unheard of at the time," he said. "I didn't think it was out of line because I was the one drawing the crowds for him. The promoter finally said, 'Okay, but you'll be sorry later.' What they did was cheat me on how many counts I'd get from the referee when I'd get thrown out of the ring. I was supposed to get twenty counts, but they only gave me ten, so it looked like I quit the fight and then they could say because I quit, I didn't get my money. Well, I demanded the money, and then this promoter and three or four of his henchmen followed me downstairs and they beat the hell out of me. A terrible beating. It was so bad, I had to come home to Des Moines and take five or six months off and was in and out of the hospital several times. I was having terrible headaches and couldn't do anything. It was almost like a mental breakdown."

Already married, already the father of one son and soon to be the father of a second, Babe Bisignano began realizing life might be better if he'd get into something besides fighting for the rest of his career.

Oh, there were a few more matches, notably with his friend Bronko Nagurski, who'd been a great college football

All-American before he went to the ring. But the fighting and wrestling years were coming to an end. Pinkie George, the old promoter who had launched him, was still around, but they'd long since had a falling-out and Babe had used other promoters.

"What happened between Babe and me," George said, "was that from the first moment he strapped on a glove, I could tell he thought he knew more about promotion than I did. Maybe he was right, but I went on to do all right for myself. But then, we were both young and feisty and would talk back to each other. I wanted some respect from him, and that's not an easy thing to get from Babe."

6

FALLING IN LOVE

"...more class in he

ttle toe than. . .in my
hole body."

PINKIE GEORGE may have had trouble getting respect from Babe, but there was one person who didn't—Catherine Dwyer Bisignano, a shy beauty who met him in 1931, married him in 1933, bore him five children, worked as hard at home as he did at the restaurant, and eventually died at the age of seventy-two in 1979 after an agonizing fifteen-year battle with cancer.

"Babe was married to a woman who did a lot to straighten him out," Pinkie George said. And at a fortieth-anniversary-of-business roast held for Babe a decade ago, Msgr. William McMahon had his predinner prayer interrupted by loud applause when he thanked the Lord "for the presence of Catherine Bisignano in this millionaire busboy's life."

Babe says, "She had more class in her little toe than I've ever had in my whole body."

He first saw her when he was eighteen and waiting for a bus in downtown Des Moines. She was twenty-three, on her way to work as a clerk in a Fanny Farmer candy shop. "She was the most beautiful thing you've ever seen in your whole life," he said. "She was prematurely gray, and she had the most beautiful complexion that any woman ever had.

"I knew who her best friend was, Mary DeCorpo, so I asked Mary to get me a date with Catherine. She said Catherine had never dated, and that she doubted she'd go out with me. But I asked her, and she was kind of a wrestling fan, so she decided to. We started dating quite a bit.

"She lived with her father, John Dwyer, who was a big Irishman, and I'll never forget when he found out she was going out with me. She took me over there to introduce me, and he turned his back on me. I don't think he thought much of Italians in the first place, and he didn't like wrestlers, either."

But they married, and she joined him on the big-time wrestling circuit, riding a bus all night long from Des Moines to meet him in New York City.

What followed were three years of fun together, as they roamed the nation's major cities where Babe was wrestling. She became involved in the hype associated with wrestling cards by appearing in newspaper photos wearing that day's version of a miniskirt and putting wrestling holds on her husband. And she was often photographed patching one of his swollen eyes or feeding him a plate of spaghetti.

"She was such a knockout that everywhere we'd go—whether it was Fifth Avenue in New York or Hollywood Boulevard out in California—when we'd walk down the street together, all the men would be turning around to get another look at her," Babe said. "Made me proud. She didn't change much over the years, either—not really with the kids and not really when we started making some real money. I was always an extreme extrovert. Now, I wouldn't say she was an introvert, but she was more just a plain, good, wholesome mother.

"Even after we did get some money, you'd really never

have known that she had a dime. She didn't have furs and she didn't have diamonds, even though she could have had as much of that stuff as she wanted. Her only big luxury deal was her big, blue Cadillac. She loved having that, and she always had it full of nuns going to this or going to that. She did so much work for Mercy Hospital and things like that that you wouldn't believe it. She put in the first snack shop down there and ran it for a while, and all of us would get down there and help clean it—the kids more than me, I guess, because I was always busy cleaning the restaurant.

"I can remember way back there, she had this pair of blue tennis shoes that were her favorite thing to wear around home. No one else wore those kinds of shoes back then when they went out in public, and one day, she said she had to run over to the grocery store and she asked me if I thought she could wear those shoes for something like that. I told her, 'Katy, with the money you've got, you could walk into that grocery store barefooted if you wanted to.' But she always worried about things like that." You'll notice he called her Katy there. He alternately called her Catherine, Katy, Kay, and Mom. She almost always called him Babe.

"In a lot of ways, I guess we didn't have a normal husband and wife relationship, primarily because I was always working at the restaurant until two or three in the morning," he said. "But, believe me, she worked just as hard at home as I did downtown, just different hours because of doing all the kid things. I'd come home and she'd usually be asleep. What fun and pleasure she should probably have gotten from me, she found a lot of that in the kids. There was just never a better mother, ever. You can't believe how devoted she was to those kids and to the grandkids.

"We never did a lot together, never went on many vacations. I didn't think there was time, and maybe that was a mistake, but I was always doing what I had to do. I do remember one vacation where we got this new station wagon, loaded all the kids up, and took off for California. Those kids would get to fighting, and I'd go crazy. I remember stopping once in the middle of the desert, getting out of the car and running as hard as I could out into the middle of nowhere just because I couldn't stand it anymore. I was never so glad to get home. She handled those things so much better than I did. She'd just take everything in stride."

Oh, there were arguments—were there ever!

Joe Bisignano, their first-born, now fifty-two and still living in Des Moines, said he thinks "the marriage was solid. I don't think either one of them ever thought about leaving the other, like happens so much in today's society, but they would argue. It was usually over us kids or the business."

John Bisignano, forty-two and the youngest, now lives in Breckenridge, Colorado. He looks back on his parents as being "very close, not terribly affectionate but not unaffectionate, either. They did fight like cats and dogs, but never with violence, just with arguments. But let's remember one thing," he continued. "Katy was a full-blooded Irishman, and she loved to fight. Sometimes I'm sure Dad didn't even want to fight, but she'd get him backed so far into a corner that there wasn't anything he could do but fight. But the good thing about it was that they never seemed to come to hate each other over it. I don't know, maybe they both found some kind of emotional common ground when they were going through those fights."

Jim Bisignano, forty-nine and living in Birmingham, Michigan, recalls that "Mom was the family person. With Dad being gone so much, she had to play both roles as father and mother a lot of times. She handled the kid problems, and she handled them well. She instilled the things in me that have made me the father I like to think I am today. An intense devotion to family. Oh, don't get me wrong. She wasn't one to 'spare the rod.' She was a very strict disciplinarian, and I want to tell you, you didn't want to get in the way of her backhand if you screwed up."

Judy Bisignano, forty-six, a nun who lives and teaches in Tucson, Arizona, and who will be referred to from now on as Sister Judy, looks back on "a lot of Dad's 'Italianness' being part of their relationship. "I think he adored Mom, but he didn't have a real reservoir of tenderness. He now glorifies her in death, which is also part of being Italian. He always thought tenderness was weakness. We kids and grandkids were everything for her in that way," Sister Judy said. "I think Mom loved him, but I also think she accepted him for what he was and what he wasn't. She loved him, but more, she accepted him."

There were, all of the kids are certain, many times when Catherine Bisignano just had to be embarrassed by her husband's public antics—Babe going to jail, newspaper articles on how he roughed up somebody on a Des Moines street, Babe drinking too much and making a buffoon of himself at a big dinner, Babe being Babe.

"That stuff would worry her, all right," Babe said. "But she didn't realize that some of the things I done, I had to do. I had to fight my way up, and I had to fight to stay on top. She didn't know the politics, the jealousy I had to deal with. The war was on, and I had to bootleg to stay in business. But a lot of times, she didn't understand."

Sister Judy thinks her mother understood more than Babe realized. "I can remember one time when he was emceeing something, got too much to drink, and started telling off-color jokes," she said. "I was sitting with Mom, and I asked her if he embarrassed her. She said, 'No, he'd be embarrassed for himself if he was smart enough. But that's his problem, not mine. I am not a reflection of him.' I think all of us eventually adopted that kind of an attitude about it."

There were rumors over the years, some more persistent than others, about Babe having an affair with another woman, not a one-night fling but a long-term sort of thing. In that often-loose time of World War II, with the nightclub atmosphere and with Babe's celebrity, there must have been opportunities.

"That's a fucking lie!" Babe roared, when I asked him. It is of note that he used a word there that he almost never, ever uses, even though he commonly uses lots of other blue ones.

"I never had an affair with anyone. That's the kind of bullshit all of us in this business always had to put up with. You fire some waitress, and then you start hearing all the talk, and your wife starts getting phone calls about it at two and three in the morning. That stuff just goes with this business." First telling me to "go ahead and give me your best hold on this, check it out, talk to anybody you want," he later became so angry about it that he stopped giving interviews or information.

Sister Judy doubted there was ever any infidelity on either side of the marriage, saying, "None of us kids knew anything about that happening, and I know one thing, if Dad had tried something like that, Mom would have killed him."

That's right, said Babe in his last word on the matter. "There would have been no second chances for me with Katy."

Johnnie Stamatelos, a long-time friend and competitor at his Johnnie's Vets Club in West Des Moines, doubts any Babe affair, too. "I never knew of him doing anything like that ever," Stamatelos said, "and I've known the guy forever. I've been drunk with him, even in Vegas—and if you were going to try to pull something, it'd be there, right? I'll tell you the truth. When it comes to chasing broads, the guy has been a square. For some reason, he was nuts about his wife. The world's biggest square on that."

One thing is certain, there was deep love there at the end. "When she was on her deathbed, I couldn't get away for even a couple of minutes without her saying, 'Where's Babe? Where's Babe?' And I didn't want to get away, either. I've been miserable ever since she died. God, I miss her."

Catherine Dwyer Bisignano.

*L*ife in the Bisignano household was really
run by Babe's wife, Catherine, who died from
cancer in 1979. They had five children: Joe,
Jim, Mary Kay, Judy, and John. It was a plush
childhood, complete with child-size motorized
cars. There were visits from the nation's
famous, as when Frank Leahy spent the night
and posed for a photo with all the Bisignano
little ones. "I can't think of another family so
much different in the way it's been raised from
the way their father was raised than in this
situation," Babe said. "My family doesn't know
me." The kids disagree.

Notre Dame football coach Frank Leahy with the Bisignano kids.

With Joe and Jim, after a father-son golf tournament.

With daughter Mary Kay.

With Catherine and daughter Judy.

The Bisignano kids in recent times (Joe and Jim in back and Sister Judy and John in front).

7

BABE AND HIS KIDS

"...they never wen

hrough what I did."

THE BABE BISIGNANO SHOW, I've called it. And as it plays on, it's hard to know whether to call it a comedy or a tragedy. Higher highs and lower lows than normally exist in several lifetimes all come to play in the singular life of this simple, yet complex, man.

Nowhere do they come to play stronger than in his relationship—or rather lack of one—with his four grown children. (Another daughter, Mary Kay, was born third in line. She died at age twenty-three in 1964 from Hodgkin's disease, taking her vows as a nun on her deathbed in Dubuque.) On the one hand, he is uncommonly proud of them. "There isn't one of the four who isn't more successful in the careers they are in than I've ever been in mine," he said. That is pretty much true.

Joe is one of the most successful and respected stockbrokers in Des Moines.

Jim is an acclaimed artist who works from his studio in Michigan and whose paintings are big-ticket pieces that hang in prominent places coast to coast.

Sister Judy holds a doctorate in education and has founded and still directs an innovative private school in Tucson, the Kino Learning Center, for elementary and high school students. Arizona Senator Dennis DeConcini calls her

65

"certainly one of the finest educators anywhere in the United States and for sure in this state." Babe has generously backed her financially in that effort, even once buying her a school bus. Sister Judy responded by having "Babe's My Pal" painted on it, using the same slogan her father has used on buttons and balloons he gives to kids at his restaurant.

John, from his base in Colorado, drove Grand Prix Formula One race cars for nine years and now travels the Grand Prix circuit worldwide, acting as a commentator for racing telecasts on the ESPN sports network.

They all refer to Babe today as "Our Founder, The Mule," sometimes admiringly for his decades of hard work and sometimes disparagingly for his legendary stubbornness.

The Mule, while proud of his children is, on the other hand, uncomfortably bitter about them. Since the 1979 death of matriarch Catherine, who bonded the family together, Babe and the kids seldom see each other, seldom talk to each other.

Babe has often said loudly, and publicly, "I won't leave them a dime." But he confided in our interviews, "Oh, I probably won't stick to that because I know it'd hurt Kay if she was alive, and there's nothing I'd do to hurt her."

He points out that long ago he established an irrevocable trust on another piece of property he owns in downtown Des Moines and that that trust has been providing the kids as a group forty-eight thousand dollars per year. Ask them, he said, "why most of them haven't been home for more than three or four days in the nine years since their mother died. Ask them that.

"Yes, I'm proud of them for what they've done and are doing, but listen, who made a lot of these things possible for them? I've done more for them than what a father should do. I've done more than my share. They're all scared of me for some reason. It seems like they fear me. Good God, I'm the

biggest chicken there is, if the truth is known. I cry at anything, any time I see people in trouble. Why would they fear
me?

"I'd say my kids don't know me at all today. I think one of
the reasons we don't see eye to eye on a lot of things is because they never went through what I did. I can't think of
another family so much different in the way it's been raised
from the way their father was raised than in this situation.
My family doesn't know me. They absolutely don't know
their father."

Whoa, the kids unanimously say. They know him all too
well. They praise him for all the material things he gave
them, and for some things they say are more important—his
example of hard work and his sense of caring for the less
fortunate. "One of the best things he gave me was a sense of
'street smarts,' and I didn't have to go out in the streets to
learn it," said Joe. "I learned it from him."

They all love him and long for him. But they are weary of
their visits, infrequent as they have been, turning into confrontations and "ending on a sour note," said Joe. "Dad
might have a legitimate complaint against the family regard-
ing never coming home. There was a lot of communication
and visiting and phone calls when Mom was alive. Since
then, it's been barely a maintenance level of communication,
which isn't right." Still he again talked about "the tension
and anxiety" that seem to result from family get-togethers.

Said Jim: "Why aren't we closer? Beats me. Why don't I
come home more often? I answer that with a question—Why
was I told not to come home on his seventy-fifth birthday
when I already had a plane ticket? The gist of it had something to do with [the fact] that I hadn't come home for any
other birthdays, so why was I trying to make a big deal out of
this one?"

And Sister Judy: "It's almost a nonexistent relationship,

and that's painful. He's not a bad man at all, but he can't really meet my emotional needs because no one ever met his as a child. He's a victim of that environment he grew up in. The emotional bank is bankrupt for him, I think. His way of saying 'I love you' is saying 'I gave you the best.' He did that, too, but sometimes that's not enough. If I was to say to someone in Des Moines that we feel our father can't show love and affection and tenderness, they'd argue because they know of all the good he's done for other people. They can't understand what we're talking about. It's almost like Dad is more loved by the people of Des Moines than by his family, which is a sad commentary, isn't it?"

And John: "People can only take so many years of his bullshit. They'll only listen to that for so long before they say, 'Babe, I just don't want to hear that anymore.' That's what his true friends do, but then a lot of times they don't wind up being very long-term friends with him because he doesn't handle hearing that well."

This is perhaps too heavy for a public airing, and yet the pain that father and children share, but don't share, is so much a part of what they all are today that it would be impossible and dishonest not to mention it, particularly when all of them talk about it so openly. They do so, they say, in hopes that it can lead to some kind of reconciliation, sorrowfully adding that they question whether one can ever occur.

It's both fascinating and sad to hear them describe each other. In Sister Judy's estimation, Babe is "real tenacious, bull-headed, or maybe you say self-preserving and full of drive." In Babe's estimation, Sister Judy is "kind of a roughneck like her Dad." Sister Judy would probably say she isn't quite the "wimpo" that she says each of her brothers is from time to time. Actually, the three Bisignano boys seem to be sensitive types, not the roughnecks that Dad and Sister

Judy are. But Jim says that young John has always been a little more inclined to toughness: "Dad's paramount rule has always been you never talk back to your father. We've hardly ever done that, but for the few times we have, we've never been forgiven. Judy and John have done a lot more of that than Joe and I have. They're a lot like him, kind of chips off the old blockhead."

Part of the problem certainly must be the mix of the explosive, emotion-packed Irishness of Catherine Dwyer Bisignano and the hard-headed, self-pitying, misery-seeking Italianness of Alphonse Bisignano. Babe exhibits his end of that, to be sure, and the kids all feel the volatile mix that was bred into them.

But more important are two other factors. One is that Babe was seldom around when the children were in their formative years, a fact that he recognizes and regrets, but with the caveat, "I was working all those hours to give them more than I had when I was their age. But it was probably a mistake. I never went hunting with them. I never went fishing with them. I should have."

The other factor is his total frustration that none of his children decided to join him and ultimately take over the tremendous business that he spent over a half-century to build from nothing. And now his grandchildren are coming in for scourgings from him on the same matter.

What was it like growing up in the shadow of a man who had so quickly become the best-known character in Iowa and beyond, a man who was hardly ever around home when the kids were?

John Bisignano said he's often been dumbstruck by how far his father's fame, or notoriety, has spread. "It's happened to me all over the world," he said. "I call them my 'Are you Babe's boy?' stories. One of the best was that in those years when I was driving race cars my life's dream was to drive in the Grand Prix on the streets of Monte Carlo. So after three or four years, I finally qualified, so there I am driving in there to register with my car on a trailer, and I'm dressed to the hilt as the successful young race car driver, sort of my Paul Newman image. I get into Monte Carlo, get out of the truck, walk up to the registration table, and give my credentials to this little French guy. He starts looking them over, looks up at me, and says, 'Are you Babe's boy?' It turned out this guy had worked for about six months at the Hotel Fort Des Moines while he was on a tour of America, and he'd met my Dad. I about fell over.''

Growing up in the Bisignano household and living with a legend was hardly ever bad, the kids all say, and it was often fun and was always cushy. And the only thing bad about it from Babe's end, he said, was that "Katy couldn't tell them no. I was the one who had to come in and say no, or ground them, or take the car away. I look back on that and I think sometimes I was kind of made out to be the bulldog. Maybe that's part of why things are like they are now.''

The huge Bisignano home on Forty-third Street in the affluent west central part of Des Moines, where Babe still lives, was always comfortable, indeed luxurious. It was the neighborhood hangout for all the kids, the favorite stop on Halloween night. One year Catherine handed out six hundred candy apples to the visiting goblins.

There were visits by the famous. Frank Leahy, who was the head football coach at Notre Dame, once spent a night with the family and played with the kids.

There was plenty of music. "They all took piano lessons,'' Babe said, "and it seemed like we always had a saxophone and accordian around. I can remember we started Sister Judy playing the violin, but she hated it. She hated it so bad when she'd get up there on stage to play it in the school programs, she'd be so mad her face would turn bright red.''

There were always dogs.

"I don't like dogs, never liked dogs, but we always had one," Babe said. "And they ate good, too—scraps of steak from the restaurant. Well, one time we had this boxer named Sparky. At the time this happened, I was home recovering from surgery, and I'm in bed. But this kid who'd been over at our house had walked home and Sparky had followed him most of the way. The problem was that when they got close to this kid's home, Sparky did something in this guy's yard, and the guy came out and grabbed Sparky and locked him up in his garage. So the little boy called us and told us.

"I got madder than hell, so I got up out of bed to go get my dog. Joe happened to be home from Notre Dame, so he said he'd go, too. And Katy said she was going along to keep us out of trouble. So I go over there and knock on this guy's door and decide I'm going to try to scare him. I said, 'I'm Babe Bisignano, and what the hell are you doing with my dog locked up in your garage?' Now, this is a great big guy I'm talking to. He said, 'Your dog poo-pooed in my yard!' I couldn't stand it. If he'd said, 'Your dog shit in my yard,' that would have been different. So I said, 'Well, if you don't give me my dog, I'm going to poo-poo you right in the mouth!' Then I went back to his garage, found a piece of pipe, and started trying to break the lock on the door so I could get Sparky out of there.

"This guy called the police, of course, and the officer came and tried to calm everything down. At one point, I was saying again that I was going to poo-poo this guy right in the mouth, and it looked like there might be trouble. That's when I looked over and I noticed that Joe was taking off his Notre Dame jacket and hanging it on a fence post.

"Later, I said to him that I appreciated him doing that— that he was willing to jump in and help the old man. But Joe said that when he thought there was going to be trouble, what he was really doing was taking off that jacket with 'Notre Dame' written on it 'because I didn't want to disgrace Our Blessed Mother.' What a great kid, huh?"

So what about Sparky? "I guess we finally got him back,"

said Babe, "but, you know, I can't remember for sure."

And speaking of dogs, it is impossible not to tell the tale of how Babe once "fixed" a dog show. "We always had good dogs, papers on them and all that," he said. "We had this one little dog, and there was this big dog show coming up in town. Little Johnny was showing him, and the night before the show these people came into the restaurant and I found out they were going to be the judges the next day. So I bought them dinner and a bunch of drinks and told them about my dog. What the hell, there's nothing wrong with trying to fix a little dog show, is there?

"So the next day, we go there, and Johnny is showing the little dog. The guy next to us was displaying two or three hundred ribbons his dog had won, so I knew it was going to be pretty tough. But I also knew that we had a pretty good chance of winning something. The way it turned out, the judges created some special class for our dog and then gave us a third place ribbon, but that was good enough for me."

The Bisignano kids always had everything—good clothes, flashy cars, motorcycles. John can even remember having "my own boat on the Des Moines River when I was fourteen years of age.

"But that gets into what was one of the best things Dad taught us. He always showed us it was nice to have things, but that we absolutely had to work for them and even more important, we had to share them. On that boat, I remember coming home and Dad would say, 'Who did you take out with you today? You let them ski, too, didn't you? You didn't do all the skiing yourself, did you?' He was teaching all of us that even though you have a lot, you're not better than anybody else. And we'd see him doing that himself over and over. We'd see him down at the restaurant sitting down to eat a plate of spaghetti with the dishwasher guy, and we'd see him coming in off the street with some bum who was half-frozen. He'd sit them down next to the pizza ovens for a few minutes to let them thaw out and then he'd be giving them a prime rib dinner. I don't think any of us have ever forgotten how Dad's

72

always been like that, and we're trying to do the same things."

Sister Judy said for all they had, "I never got the idea we were wealthy—we just never acted like that around home—until I got into high school and started running into some bigotry because of it. But by then, I could handle it. I knew we weren't any better."

The girls were good athletes at St. Augustin School and then at St. Joseph Academy. They still hold some records in Catholic youth athletic leagues. The boys were never big enough to be forces in Dowling sports, but they still tried and Babe recognizes today that "they probably kept trying just for me because they knew that sports have always been important to me." He said his proudest moment as the father of a boy athlete occurred when Joe, who was a shrimp of a punter for Dowling, kicked the ball against East High, ran down the field so fast he got out of control, jumped on the pile of tacklers, and wound up getting a fifteen-yard penalty for unnecessary roughness. "I loved that," Babe said. "He was the littlest player on the field getting stuck for unnecessary roughness. That's my boy."

Just as the famous and notorious were often guests in the Bisignano home, so were the religious. "Sometimes it seemed like we were running almost a halfway house for priests and nuns," Babe said. "They were always around here. It was like they could come here, get away from church for a while, have a drink if they wanted to, and just relax. We got to know a lot of them, and they meant a whole lot to us."

And he thinks their presence had an impact on the decisions of daughters Mary Kay and Judy to become nuns.

Mary Kay was the older of the two. Unlike "roughneck" Judy, Mary Kay "was more like her mom, quiet and reserved and a lot of class," Babe said. "And in her last year of high school, we started noticing a change in her. She finally said she really wanted to go to the convent, and we were thrilled.

"She went through all the application process to join the order of the Sisters of the Blessed Virgin Mary in Dubuque and got accepted. About then, the family had a trip scheduled to the shrine in Lourdes, and so we had to get passports and shots and physicals. When Mary Kay went through that, the doctors noticed a swelling in the neck. We didn't know what it was at first, but then they came back and diagnosed it as Hodgkin's disease. They said she'd have two or three years to live. We were crushed, worse than anything I've ever been through. If it hadn't been for those priests and nuns being around us all the time, we'd never have made it through this.

"There was a question, of course, about whether she could go ahead and join the sisters because you have to be in top physical health to get into a convent. So I went to Dubuque and talked to the Mother Superior and asked her to please let my daughter still come, that it meant so much to her. I assured her that Mary Kay, because of her illness, would never be a financial drain on them because I would take care of that. The Mother Superior said that wouldn't even matter, that she already had been accepted and that they were expecting her to come.

"So she went over there and went through it all, even though she was gone sometimes for medical treatment. We tried everything for her. We kept thinking there must be some doctor somewhere who could do something. She went through five long years of pain and suffering, but she also completed her work. And she took her vows when she was on her deathbed."

Mary Kay's story represents two of the proudest moments in Babe Bisignano's life. First, there was the fact that she saw it through to become a nun. But there was something else that happened—something very un-Babelike—and it happened on the day she was leaving Des Moines to go to Dubuque for the first time.

"There were about twelve girls leaving all at the same time, so we'd arranged an airplane for them to fly up there,"

74

Babe said. "We were all at the airport to see them off, and I walked up to her and said, 'Mary Kay, I promise you that I will write to you every day of our lives.' She came right back at me. She said, 'Oh, Dad, you don't like to write in the first place. And who'll help you spell?' I want to tell you something. I never, ever missed a day. Some days they were pretty short and sometimes I wrote them after I'd had too much wine or something, but I never missed a day. Not a one. That was one time in my life when I really did the right thing."

Now, twenty-four years after her death, he continues to memorialize her. For example, he is quick to point out that Mary Kay was so special and so courageous that the doctor in Dubuque who took care of her named his own daughter after her. Babe maintains Mary Kay's picture, along with ones of Sister Judy and of several of his favorite priests, on the wall in front of the kneeler in his den where each day he pauses to say the Rosary. And he's already given $23,000 toward a $125,000 sculpture that will stand as a memorial to her on the campus of Clarke College in Dubuque, where he is a member of the board of trustees.

Babe is close to only one of his nine grandchildren— Jim's daughter, Mary Kay, who is studying for a master's degree in dance at UCLA. Babe is helping put her through school. Why are they so close?

"I think a lot of it is that we write back and forth all the time, and I'm the only one of the grandkids who does that with him," said Mary Kay, who is twenty-six. "But the truth is that I think Grandpa felt something special for me, even before we started writing. I think it was because I was named after his daughter, and she has such a special place in his heart. I think he's definitely a good man. I think sometimes he's afraid to show people what a good man he is. He's got that tough guy thing, you know."

What do the other grandkids think of her special relationship with him? "I think they probably have some negative feelings, but not toward me," she said. "My siblings think I'm lucky. I guess they probably think it's unfortunate that he doesn't have as fond of a feeling toward the rest of them. But they think that's more something to do with Babe than it is to do with them."

At the bottom of the matter, without doubt, is the restaurant. Just as he's done with his own kids, especially the boys, Babe raises hell about how none of his grandchildren have come to work for him. "Why wouldn't I resent it," he said, "when I've got granddaughters who go to work at other Des Moines restaurants but they won't work for me?"

This is where Babe takes a major hit. For few people who know the situation, those who know it from being friends and counselors and being on the inside, agree with him.

"You want to know why none of them—the kids or the grandkids—work for him?" said Fred Eckrosh, the longtime friend who worked thirty years for him. "It's because he's run them off, that's why. He's a bear to work for, and he doesn't need to be. In a lot of ways, he's a smart man, and in a lot of ways, he's a terrific dummy."

And listen to his brother, Chuck, who has his own successful restaurant: "On this stuff about the kids, I disagree with him. He wanted them in the restaurant, and they didn't want to be there. They're all intelligent and successful, the greatest kids you could find. He has no right to feel the way he does toward those kids over this restaurant. They're wonderful kids. I love them like my own. He's wrong on this, but he's the one who's making himself miserable.

"They've all done so well. What the hell does he want from them? He's wrong! Nobody agrees with him on that, especially the way he rants and raves in public about it. But that's Babe. It just makes a lot of misery and hell that shouldn't be there. But what can you do? Nobody agrees with him about it."

Babe argues that none of the kids have ever given it a chance.

76

"We all tried," Joe said. "It's just not a business that appealed to us. We all had summer jobs there as we were growing up and going to college. On Sundays we'd go in there and help clean up and stock the coolers. I spent four years with him after college, working either at the restaurant or at the meat market he owned, but it was always the family business I was working in. Four years. It's not like we've turned down something we didn't know anything about or hadn't experienced. We were all there, and we decided we wanted to do other things."

Jim agreed: "We all tried, but Dad somehow just doesn't remember that we did. Before I went on my own as an artist, I was working for General Motors in Detroit. I'd get two weeks vacation a year, and I'd usually spend at least part of that vacation busing dishes for him at the restaurant. It was never good enough.

"One time, he was going to be gone for a week for something, so I took a week off from General Motors just to come home and help at the restaurant. Now, I don't know about the restaurant business, but from working for General Motors, I had learned some general business principles. One thing I saw right away about the restaurant is that the major problem is good help, and the lower the job, the bigger the problem is. They were getting dishwashers on a daily basis, and it was always a struggle. One thing I noticed was when they'd get a kid in there one day who turned out to be pretty good, nobody was asking him how to get hold of him later in case we needed help and he wanted to work. When Dad got home, I made the mistake of suggesting that. What I got back was, 'You smart-assed son of a bitch. Who are you to tell me how to run my business? Just because you work at General Motors, do you think that means you know anything about the restaurant business?' It was pretty discouraging."

Jim said his father "has the idea Mom somehow turned us against going into the restaurant with him. That's absolutely untrue and has no basis in reality. She in fact encouraged us to take an interest in the restaurant and pointed out the financial benefits that could be there for us. She always kept reminding us that he never had really had a mother and a father and that that explained a lot about why he is like he is. She'd say you don't always have to go along with him but that you have to try to understand him. We have. You know, it could have been very easy for one of us kids to say at some point, 'To hell with you. I'm never talking to you again.' But we didn't do that because we've remembered what Mom always told us."

When John, the youngest, came along, he said, "I had five times as much pressure on me to go into the restaurant with him than the others did. I was his last big hope. I worked for him every Saturday and every holiday from the time I was fourteen years old, and even when I'd come home from college, I'd work for him on vacations. And in college, my degree was in restaurant management. I was the one being really groomed.

"My last real, serious attempt to make it work started in June of 1975. I was twenty-eight years old, an adult, and I'd been racing cars all over the world for several years. It wasn't like I'd never seen anything else. But I came back and went to work for him. It turned out to be the craziest eleven months of my life. The more work I did, the more trouble I got into. I'd get fired two to three times a week. All that is because the Babe's restaurant is really Babe himself. He'd shove anybody who was any good at working there out the door because he's so protective of it. The staff would have pools on how long a new manager would last, and the smart bet was that the more capable these people really were, the less time they'd be there. We had some of them who didn't even last through the first noon hour. Yet the ones who were no challenge to him, those who'd be like dishrags when he started ranting and raving, they'd stay on for twenty-five years and more.

"He doesn't think I did anything at that restaurant, but I did everything, and I never once fell on my ass. But it came to a point where all of a sudden, the customers and the employees started coming to me with their problems instead of to him. When he realized that, he realized that now there was more than just Babe at Babe's restaurant; now there was sort of a young Babe, too. When that hit him, I was gone. I was history. He got me out of there fast."

It is obvious, though, that the kids do indeed love him. Listen to John, after he has just unloaded here on his father: "I want to close this by telling you that I think I've got the greatest dad in the whole world. I love him more now than I've ever loved him in my life. I know that he'd cut off both his arms if he thought it would save my little finger. But we have almost no contact. I handle that by understanding it. Joe is frustrated, but he handles it. Jim and Judy are still trying to handle it from a basis of hurt instead of a basis of understanding. That's why whenever we do get together, Jim starts hyperventilating and has to go breathe into a bag and Judy has to go pound on a wall. I don't. I've come to understand why he's like that, and it gives me some peace. Do you realize he was one of the top officials of the Big Brothers and Big Sisters organization in Des Moines at a time when he wasn't talking to any of his own kids?

"That's just the way it is. We love our father. We love him dearly. None of us would be where we are without him. He just won't let us be anything except what he wanted us to be, and that doesn't mean much when we've all turned out as successful as we are. We don't come home because we hate to have confrontations with him. It's at best a very uneasy calm. It hurts us to be the brunt of his blame for his misery when we're not responsible. We're not hurting for ourselves, though. We're hurting for him because he feels like he has to blame us when we're blameless."

As for Babe's statement that he isn't going to leave them a dime—"When he says that, I say fine," said Joe, the oldest. "He made it. He ought to be able to dispose of it anyway he wants. We all had the opportunity to be part of it and have it, and we turned it down."

And a reconciliation?

"I think the first move is up to them," said Babe.

Said Joe: "I don't see it happening. Oh, maybe if he sold the restaurant there could be. Then he'd get some other interests and find out there's a life beyond that restaurant. Maybe then. But otherwise, I doubt it. Whenever we get together now, it seems like only a matter of time before the litany comes up about how none of us came in and took it over."

That's getting old, all the kids said. But all of them are, too. And so is Babe.

8

THE RESTAURANT/BAR BUSINESS

". . .you'd have to have brains to be a plumber or electrician."

THE HALF-CENTURY business success of Babe Bisignano, he says himself, has been a matter of "the right guy at the right time with a big place, a lot of hard work and a lot of luck"—and the devout prayer he knelt down and said in the restaurant's vestibule on opening day, March 25, 1939, asking God "that I could sell one keg and ten cases of beer so I could clear the twenty-five dollars a day I needed to stay open."

He opened the doors, sold the beer, and has stayed open ever since, doing up to two million dollars in business a year and rolling in dough himself.

More people have probably had their first drink, their first date, their wedding party, or their anniversary party at Babe's than at any other place in Iowa. Presidential candidates go there, stars of music and movies and media go there, and so do top coaches and athletes. And they mingle and revel in that plush atmosphere of food, drink, tradition, and a hint of naughtiness that's all wound up in the place's bootlegging past. The old bootlegger himself—or call him the millionaire busboy if you prefer—is never far away with a free drink and an outrageous story.

It was at first just a tavern. In 1941, Babe added a supper club operation. Shortly thereafter, he added the now-dead Jungle Club as a special section, finishing it in bamboo and installing illegal but very popular slot machines. In 1944, he bought the Sixth Avenue building where his downtown restaurant is still located. He was closed for most of 1947 when he spent six months in jail for his shenanigans with the law. In 1965, a fire destroyed the place. He was closed for a year but rebuilt and reopened with the fanfare you'd expect from such a showman. Along the way, he also bought Casson's meat market, mainly to ensure a good supply of quality meat during war rationing, although he eventually sold it. He's had, and still has, lucrative real estate holdings beyond the restaurant. In the fall of 1988, when he was seventy-five years old, he did something "that everybody in town thinks is crazy" and opened Babe's North, a smaller and more intimate version of his downtown operation.

"The real reason I did that is that I stayed downtown five years too long," he said. "Nobody comes downtown anymore. If it wasn't for conventions coming into town, I couldn't exist downtown today. So I've got the downtown place up for sale. I know nobody is going to buy it as a restaurant. It's just too damned big. But it is a prime piece of property. Somebody will probably build another big office building there. So I opened this place up north, and eventually I'll take my key help—the people who've been with me for years—and we'll go up there and run that little place and take it easy."

Kind of a retirement joint?

"Yeah," he said. "I've got to have a place, always." What he's thinking about is an often-repeated comment by his friend Maury White, the retired *Register* sports columnist, that "without that restaurant, Babe, you're just another rich Italian in Des Moines."

And Babe's answer? "That's right. Me without a restaurant would be like Maury White without a column. The public forgets you real quick. Look at Maury. He's been retired a few months and now nobody knows who he is."

To show how fast it happened for Babe, listen to his brother Chuck: "When I left for service overseas in 1944, Babe owed on nine loans. When I came home two years later, he was more than a millionaire." But was that start ever tough—and as if he needed more pressure, his second son was born the day after he opened.

Babe came home from the wrestling wars beat-up, determined to start a new life, and with five thousand dollars in his bank account, as he says, "a pretty good chunk of money in 1939."

Why a tavern? "Well, you'd have to have brains to be a plumber or electrician or something like that," he said. "All I had was my name. I was well known from being in the ring. That's the same thing that has happened over and over with sports people. Think about how many of them open bars or restaurants."

But check another longtime friend, Carl Cacciatore, a successful businessman himself: "Babe always talks about how dumb he is, but if I had to put money on someone dealing with money, it'd be Babe. He knows what he's doing."

The five thousand dollars, however, was not going to be enough to rent the place on Sixth, refurbish it with nice leather booths, and buy the necessary opening supply of beer. Remember, hard liquor was not a factor early on. There was no liquor by the drink then in Iowa. If you wanted a shot of real booze, you had to buy your own bottle and take it to a "key club," where you'd be charged for the mix, the glass, and the ice.

So he started approaching banks for a twenty-five-hundred-dollar loan. "I got turned down by two of them," he said. "The first one I went to, they asked what I had as 'collateral.' It's bad enough when you don't have any, but it's even worse when you don't even know what the word means. When they explained to me that they wanted me to have some assets that they could base the loan on, I said, 'Good God! If I had all that, I wouldn't be in here asking for a twenty-five-hundred-dollar loan!' I don't think they thought I was a very good risk."

A loan officer at a third bank, however, said he would consider Babe's application overnight. "I'll tell you, Katy and I went home that night, gave the Rosaries a workout, prayed to St. Jude and everything else," Babe said. "And the next morning, they said they would give me a loan. But they stuck a special deal on me. They said they'd give me five separate five-hundred-dollar loans, and that I had to go get five cosigners on each loan, and that nobody could be a cosigner on more than one of them.

"I thought that was just the way they operated, but the first guy I went to told me the bank was just using another way to turn me down because I wouldn't be able to find twenty-five people to cosign. But I did. I didn't know any big shots, those South-of-Grand people. The ones who signed for me were my people, the little people who'd known me forever. I think they're all gone now. I think I've buried them all. But I've never forgotten them."

The loan and four other things really launched him: (1) his personality; (2) an early visit by the fans of the St. Ambrose College football team, who were in Des Moines from Davenport to watch their Fighting Bees play the Drake Bulldogs in football; (3) the arrival of fifteen thousand trainees for the Women's Army Corps during World War II; and (4) that old passion, learned in the poverty of his boyhood, to "make a buck."

What could the St. Ambrose College football fans have to do with it?

"They came in for that football game, and keep in mind they came from Davenport, which is a Mississippi River town and was as wide open as river towns usually are for booze and stuff like that," Babe said. "They came in before the game and had some beers, but they really wanted booze. I told them I couldn't serve it. So they went out and bought several bottles of liquor and brought them back to me. They said they'd be back after the game and that I should just serve them drinks out of those bottles and charge them a regular price. Well, I did that, and I never saw so much money come into the cash register so quick and easy. I thought to myself, 'My God, where have I been?' "

Thereafter, Babe started selling booze illegally—even in coffee cups if the "heat" happened to be on—and his business boomed.

But it was the war and the presence of all those WACs in Des Moines "that really made me," he said. "We'd sell more booze on a Saturday night then than we sell in a month now. They were training at Fort Des Moines out on the south side, but they also took over several of the hotels downtown. When they were early in their training, they had to stay right there, but I want to tell you, when they'd get their first night off, this town would be jumping."

He catered to them, oh did he ever.

"I was 4F in the draft myself because of ulcers," he said, "but I think I did my part. I kept an awful lot of them happy. I'll tell you, none of them ever left my joint hungry or dry just because they didn't happen to have money. When they had to be back at midnight, sometimes some of them would miss the last streetcar, but I'd have one of my guys out there with my Cadillac taking them back. And some of those gals didn't get enough time to go shop, so they'd leave me an order. I'd send one of the waitresses over to Younkers and we'd buy all these brassieres and panties and have them all ready to go when the gals came back in the next time.

"I think they liked it. At least I know I got pictures back from all over the world where they'd put up signs like in front of their commissary there calling it 'Babe's' or they'd have a sign up saying it was so many miles to Babe's. The place got so popular that the guys in the Air Force who were flying across the country started always having 'engine trouble' when they were near Des Moines, and they'd land here and stick around for two or three days. The Air Force finally came close to putting the Des Moines Airport off-limits because of that."

One of those WACs who hung out at Babe's was Peggy Graffouliere, now eighty and living in Carmel, California. She became such a regular, in fact, that she married Babe's bandleader, the late Frenchy Graffouliere.

"Babe's was *the* place to go to then," she said. "The food was magnificent, the band was lovely, the place was beautifully decorated, and there were those double bars. Yes, we all knew he was serving booze illegally, but the laws were so stupid then that I think everybody in Iowa got drunk on purpose. It was the drinkingest place I've ever seen. All of us loved Babe. I always called him 'Big, Fat Smooch' and then after I started up with Frenchy, they became 'Big Smooch' and 'Little Smooch.' "

Ah, yes, the music, the dancing, the entertainment. In his sudden affluence, Babe started hiring such name Hollywood stars as Spike Jones, Georgie Gobel, and others. But he didn't have to go that far, or pay that much, for his biggest find.

He'd become friends with the Rev. Frederick J. Weertz, pastor of St. John's Lutheran Church, located just a block from the restaurant. Pastor Weertz, like Babe, was a former boxer. "We got so close," Babe said, "that a lot of times when I had a personal problem, I'd go talk to him instead of going to my own Catholic priests. That started me off being close to the Lutherans, and I have been ever since. I kid heck out of them, though. I always tell them, 'You Lutherans owe us Catholics. We took that snot-nosed Martin Luther kid, sent him to college and seminary, and—what the hell—he got out, saw where the real money was, and went to you folks instead of coming back to us.' "

But let's get back to entertainment here. It so happened that Pastor Weertz had an eighteen-year-old son, Louis Jacob Weertz, who was a freshman majoring in music at Drake University. The kid was not only directing the church's choir, he was also one hell of a piano player. Babe hired him, giving him his first professional job. And Louis Jacob Weertz, as you probably know, went on to become one of the world's favorite and best-known pianists, playing under the name of Roger Williams. "Autumn Leaves." "Born Free." "The Impossible Dream." He's done more than a hundred albums, and seventeen of them have gone gold.

But Babe isn't much for "long-haired" music. As far as he's concerned, the greatest song Roger Williams ever played was "The Donkey Serenade," which, Babe said, "is what he'd play down at my joint any time I walked in the door." The two have remained fast friends ever since, and when they get together, Williams usually winds up playing that serenade again for The Mule, as his kids call him.

"I really love him," said Williams, now sixty-four and living in Encino, California. "He reminds me so much of my father. Both were boxers, and both had that instantaneous temper that makes you hate them at one moment and love them to death the next. But, you know, a lot of people who really live life are that way.

"I'll never forget when Babe hired me. It was a big scandal, of course—the preacher's kid going to play in Babe's place where all that liquor was around and all those WACs were hanging out. I walked in to my father and said, 'Well, Dad, what do you think of your son being a nightclub piano player?' I'll never forget what he said. He looked up and said,

'Well, son, you take care of them on Saturday night and I'll take care of them on Sunday morning.' My Mom didn't take it quite that well, though. She wept bitter tears over this, and she wouldn't have much to do with Babe for a long, long time. But when she got older and got sick, and when he was coming by to call on her and send her flowers, she swung way around and came to think of Babe as the great guy that he is."

Way back then, Babe, who was paying this young pianist two dollars per hour and all the spaghetti he could eat, never dreamed the lad would become so successful and famous. "He was just a good dinner-hour piano player then," Babe said, "although there was something captivating about the way he played, even then. People would really listen to him. And, God, I can remember one night when we got raided while he was playing, and he was so cool that he just kept playing all the while the police were running around getting the liquor and arresting people. He didn't drink anything himself back then, and he still doesn't. When he's in town now for a concert or something, he still always comes in and has his glass of milk."

Restaurants, of course, thrive or fail not so much because of who owns them but more on the quality and dedication of the help. Babe has never found another piano player as good as the young Roger Williams, but he's had some other good employees—and a lot he'd like to forget.

The best of the best, he says, was Mary Lynch, his book-keeper for thirty-seven years, who died at age eighty-three in 1984. His operation hasn't been the same since she left. "She had the brains that I always lacked," he said. "She kept track of everything. And she had such a good sense about finances. To me, money was always just green stuff. If you bought something, even if it was a piece of property for like $150,000, you paid cash for it. When I was doing that, I didn't know anything about tax advantages and depreciation and all that. She did. If she'd been with me longer, or if somebody else had been who really understood that stuff, I'd have so much money now you wouldn't believe it. She was my right hand. Katy was my left hand, but Mary was my right and now I've lost them both."

You can look around his downtown restaurant now and see other good, loyal workers—Susie, Marie, Wanda, Fatima, and others—who've been with him more than twenty years. But, keep in mind as you do so that they are a handful among the sixty he typically has on the payroll downtown and the dozen who work at Babe's North.

"Yeah," he said, "I know I have the reputation of being one mean, old son of a bitch to work for, but you can't believe some of the stuff I've had to put up with. I'm not talking about my good ones here, but for the others, between what they eat and what they steal, I'm lucky to break even. Most people, I guess, are honest about it, but you never know which one isn't.

"Crazy stuff has happened. We had this one guy who came in to be a cook, we interviewed him and both Mary and I thought there was something unusual about the way he looked, but we couldn't figure out quite what it was. What it turned out to be was that this guy had lost an ear somehow and he had an artificial one on. The way we found out about it was that it fell in the soup one day.

"And back in the war years, when meat was rationed and we couldn't get all we needed, I had this rule for employees that nobody eats steak. Spaghetti, fine. But no steak. So I've got this short little bartender named Tony Basilio and I notice that down at one end of the bar he's got a big plate of spaghetti for himself, but when he's eating it, he's using a big knife to cut it. So I walked down there and poked around, and the guy had a big steak camouflaged under the spaghetti.

"About the same time, I had this poor waitress go to work, and so I'm watching her. She picked up her order from the kitchen and she's trying to carry a salad, a plate of spaghetti, a cup of tea, and a cheese shaker all at once. She couldn't get ahold of everything, so she stopped and stuck that cheese shaker right up in her armpit and took it out to the customer. I couldn't believe it. I finally grabbed her and said, 'You know, lady, there's only one place worse you could have stuck that cheese shaker.' She didn't last long.

"There was another waitress that I really had a problem with. One day I walked into the office, and Mary Lynch was just finishing interviewing this woman for a job and was telling her that we didn't have room for her. I knew we were looking for somebody, so I glanced at her credentials real quick and they looked good. She seemed to be a nice person, and I couldn't understand why Mary was turning her down. So I said, 'Well, you just report for work to me tomorrow.'' When she left, Mary was telling me this lady was a bum who was just looking for a few bucks to get her back to Omaha or someplace, but I told Mary she seemed all right. That next day came, and that woman was a disaster. She left dirty dishes all over her area, and she wasn't filling the water glasses or anything else. So I grabbed this pitcher full of ice water and walked over to her and said, 'Lady, you got any idea what this is for?' She took it from me and said, 'I sure do, you cranky son of a bitch,' and then she poured it right over my head in front of all the customers. They all were going crazy laughing about it, and Mary Lynch nearly died laughing about it when she found out.

"But probably the craziest thing I've ever been through happened on the day when we reopened for the first time after the fire in '65. I'd gone to Chicago and hired these three guys as chefs, and they were supposed to be great. I kept telling them how busy we were going to be, and they kept saying there'd be no problem. So lunchtime comes, and I mean we've got people lined up on the street trying to get in here. It was a mess, but we got through it.

"About two-thirty that afternoon things had slowed down and the three of them said they wanted to run back up to their apartment 'to freshen up.' I said that was fine, so they

90

leave. By four-thirty, they still weren't back and when we needed to be getting ready for dinner, they still weren't there. So I went up to their apartment, and the landlord told me they'd come in, packed up, and left! I didn't know what I was going to do. I went back to the restaurant, got on the phone, and called some of the other hotels and restaurants. Inside a half hour, I had the managers and chefs from several of them coming in to go to work for me for that night to get me by. It was probably the best staff I've ever had here at one time, even if it was just for that night. I don't forget that, either, when some other restaurant guy asks me for some help."

There have been three employees so loyal and good that Babe has bought houses for them. Others have received substantial loans. There are some in the same category who eventually took sick and couldn't work and yet he's kept them on the restaurant's Blue Cross and Blue Shield policy long after they were supposed to be removed from it. And, alas, there was one guy a couple of years ago who seemed reliable and who wanted to make a trip to California to see some relatives. Babe loaned the guy his near-new Oldsmobile station wagon, and that's the last he's seen of that employee and that car, although you better believe he's still looking for both.

Then there's Don Burt, fifty-six, who at this writing is still the bartender downtown. I say "at this writing" because Burt's position is always tenuous.

"I've fired this son of a bitch more times than George Steinbrenner has fired Billy Martin," Babe said to me at a moment when Burt was standing right beside us.

"Yeah, that's right, Babe," Burt said right back. "And now tell the man how many times I've quit, too."

This is obviously one curious relationship. Don Burt is a big, strapping, retired marine who doesn't need a job but enjoys working the twenty or so hours a week that Babe needs a bartender downtown. And he is a good bartender, save for one thing.

"You know how, most places, people will come from miles around if the bartender is pleasant and nice and fun to be around?" Babe asked. "Well, now they're coming from miles around to see my bartender because he's the biggest sourpuss there is. The only time he ever smiles is if he happens to win his bets on college football on Saturday. And if he loses them, watch out. He'll bite the customers' heads off."

I told Babe he ought to advertise and promote his place as having the sourest bartender in the territory. "Yeah, and then you know what would happen?" he said. "That son of a bitch would do nothing but stand behind that bar and smile and be polite. He's that kind of guy."

Babe still keeps a set of boxing gloves in the basement of the restaurant "just in case I need them," and there has been a time or two when his arguments with Burt have ended with the two of them marching off to the basement to physically settle their difference. But it's never come to blows yet. Babe said it's because Burt won't "come on down the stairs." Burt said it's because he doesn't like the idea of beating up on a seventy-five-year-old man.

So, why do they continue, at least at this writing, to tolerate each other?

Is there a chance, I asked Babe, that you like this guy because he's really so much like you?

"He is a little like me, you know?" Babe answered.

And, Don Burt, why do you put up with it?

"Oh," he said, "for some reason, I love that old son of a bitch and there's nothing I wouldn't do for him."

Incredible. But then most of Babe Bisignano's career has been.

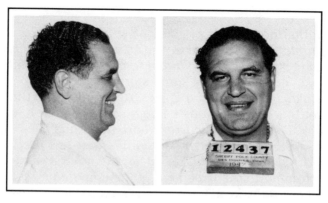

Mug shot.

*B*abe's years in business have been marked by glory and turmoil. There were the early tavern years, and then the restaurant was added. Later the Jungle Club—with its slot machines—became part of the operation. There were name entertainers, like bandleader Spike Jones. Roger Williams, who went on to become one of the world's most popular pianists, began his career at Babe's by playing during the dinner hour, despite the fact that his doing so was considered a scandal by some of his father's Lutheran church congregation. World War II, with its influx of Women's Army Corps volunteers and servicemen on furlough, was a boom time at the restaurant, where liquor was always available, even though buying it by the drink was illegal in Iowa. That ultimately put Babe in the Polk County jail, where he put in precious little time serving his six-month sentence. He filled many of the days gardening for the county and getting a suntan, and he spent most nights at home with his family. But that required that the jailers cooperate, and Babe made sure they did. Indeed, the night before his sentence expired, he threw a farewell banquet for his jailmates, having all the food and drink catered in.

By 1963, Iowa had changed its liquor laws to allow liquor by the drink, and when that happened, Babe celebrated with his most loyal employees and friends. His restaurant, in the years since, has been a gathering spot for priests and nuns, as well as the public, with Babe never far away with a free drink, a good story, or some kind of tomfoolery. In recent years, he's maintained the same stormy relationship he's always had with employees, acknowledging that "I've got this reputation as being a son of a bitch to work for." Don Burt, his current bartender, has been "fired more times than George Steinbrenner has fired Billy Martin," Babe said. The two of them have sometimes retreated to the basement of the downtown restaurant where Babe keeps two sets of boxing gloves just in case he needs to settle something with a disgruntled worker or customer. Yet, he finds himself surrounded by nearly a half-dozen waitresses who have stuck with him for more than twenty years.

The Jungle Club.

Babe and his two oldest sons, Joe and Jim, with famed bandleader Spike Jones.

One of Babe's early finds, pianist Roger Williams.

World War II times in Babe's.

Serving time.

With three
Polk County
deputies
while doing
his "jail
sentence."

The "banquet" Babe (center, back row) had catered
in at the county jail on the last night he spent
there.

Giving a hot foot to customer Al DeCarlo.

Above: Welcoming liquor by the drink with employee Fred Eckrosh. Left: Celebrating legal booze, with trusted employee Mary Lynch and pal Carl Cacciatore.

101

Babe's place, always a hangout for Catholic priests and nuns.

Aftermath of the 1965 fire that destroyed the downtown restaurant.

With bookkeeper Mary Lynch.

Mixing it up with bartender Don Burt.

With the loyal waitresses who've long carried him.

9

THE SCRAPES WITH THE LAW

"Guess who you've

got sitting
down here in jail?"

BABE BISIGNANO is a troubled man. You've
seen it in his family troubles. You've seen it about
his youth, his education, his boxing and wrestling, and his restaurant.

No stranger to trouble is he, for sure. And, yes, it seems
like it's always been that way. Why?

"A lot of times, he's his own worst enemy," said Fred
Eckrosh, the old friend and employee. "A lot of times, he'll
run his mouth when he shouldn't. He drinks excessively at
times. He's a clown at heart. But take all that, and even so,
when you get him away from that restaurant he can be the
greatest guy you've ever been around."

The trouble has been as recent as last summer, when
Polk County sanitarian Jason Petersen walked in for an in-
spection of Babe's downtown restaurant and dinged him bad
for unsanitary conditions, including food temperature problems, cockroaches, and piles of junk equipment in the basement. Petersen gave Babe a 55 rating on a scale of 100
points—and the story broke right after another Des Moines

restaurant with a 76 rating was forced to close when a bunch of customers developed salmonella poisoning.

Babe was at first as furious as he normally is when he thinks he's been crossed, raving to friends about how he'd been jobbed by "this young punk of an inspector." But, after a hearing was held on the matter, Babe was properly repentant. He put his crew to work, cleaned the place up properly, and in a reinspection in September, was given a 96 rating. He was so proud you'd have thought he'd been handed an honorary degree from his beloved Notre Dame.

Serious trouble is as ancient as the first mention in the voluminous old clippings about him in the *Des Moines Register* library.

An October 1933 story is headlined **Babe Carnera Pleads Guilty—Wrestler Is Sentenced on Fighting Charge.** Here it is in its entirety:

> Babe Carnera, 20, of 2015 Motley St., wrestler, pleaded guilty Monday to a charge of disturbing the peace by fighting. He was given a suspended sentence of three days in jail by Municipal Judge Jordan.
>
> At the time of his arrest, Carnera told police, a man had been 'saying things' about him and that he had an opportunity to 'clip' him. So he did.

What came later were more fistfights, bribes of police officers and other public officials, public shouting matches, and police raids, the shoving of a judge that resulted in a six-month jail term, coming up with phony stamps to buy meat in the time when it was being rationed, and much, much more.

Most of it can be traced back to the fact he was selling liquor illegally, which he said he had to do to stay in business and which he didn't mind doing "because the laws were stupid. If it was legal and all right in all the states around us, why was it so bad here?" he said. "Besides, I never could have sold any of it if there wasn't a demand. The people wanted it, and I got it for them."

Clark Mollenhoff, a lawyer who became a Pulitzer Prize–winning reporter for the *Register* and now is a college professor in Virginia, covered a lot of Babe's troubles back then, even though he was a college student and football player at Drake University and was just working for the paper part-time.

"When those things would come up in court," Mollenhoff said, "Babe always had this attitude that he felt he should have some sort of 'easement' on these laws because, as he always said, he was 'running a class joint' and providing almost a service to Iowans. This wasn't immoral in his mind, it was just a matter of some 'technical violations' of the law."

Things went all right for a time after his opening in 1939 and his addition of the supper club in '41. "On the booze, the heat would come and go, depending on which politicians were in charge," Babe said. "Sometimes we could run wide open, and other times we had to stop completely or start serving it in coffee cups and really hiding it. But I knew it was going to catch up to me sooner or later, because my success was killing some of these other pinheads around here. That was the jealousy I had to put up with."

We can get a sample of that in a *Des Moines Tribune* clipping from July 1943, the year when trouble started getting more serious.

> Patrolman Mose Clayman came around the corner of Seventh St. and Grand Ave. at 1:20 a.m. Tuesday and found the operators of two top-flight Des Moines night clubs, rolling around on the sidewalk, locked in combat.

The story went on to identify them as Babe Bisignano and

H. Ward Benson, operator of Benson's Dinner Club. Patrolman Clayman reported that "Bisignano was on top and had his arm around Benson's neck."

The tiff had developed when the two ran into each other at the Chesterfield Club, the story said, adding: "Bisignano has never been particularly popular with other tavern operators here and some of them have been blaming him for the present temporary cessation of gambling and sale of hard liquor downtown."

Later testimony in court had it that at the Chesterfield Club, Benson had said loudly when he saw Babe coming in, "There goes the guy who thinks he runs this town." And Babe is said to have walked over to Benson's table and said, "I understand you don't like this dago," referring to himself. Then Babe issued the invitation for Benson to join him on the street, where patrolman Clayman found them.

The fascinating thing about Bisignano is that he has always been able to go so quickly from being perceived as a public brute—whether innocent or guilty—to being perceived as a saint of a man with the public's best interest and welfare beating foremost in his heart.

Like in February of 1944, a scant few months after his brawl, when he led an effort by twenty-five Des Moines tavern operators to sell war bonds and thus support America's war effort. Babe, doing a flashback to his youth, set up a shoe shine stand downtown, hired an orchestra to back him, and had the high and mighty of Des Moines coming by to get their shoes shined and make their contributions. He raised $121,175 in a matter of hours.

Trouble for Babe hit its zenith between 1945 and 1947, in an episode that simply wouldn't happen today, or at least wouldn't come out the way it did then. When the Babe Bisignano saga is retold decades from now, this is the part of it that will get the most attention.

In late 1945, the heat was on for bootleggers. Babe's place was raided several times, and he had two booze charges pending against him in Municipal Court. (My retelling of this is based on Babe's recollections, old newspaper clippings, and interviews of others involved and around at the time.) There is an important piece of background information to know, according to Babe. A certain Municipal Court judge—not the Judge Harry Grund you're going to meet in a few moments—was one of Babe's good customers. He was such a good and loyal and regular customer, in fact, "that about once a month for a year or two he was screwing my lady piano player on my office desk right there in the restaurant," Babe said. "He was kind of a short, fat guy, and he'd come out of that office sweating and panting so bad that I was afraid he would have a heart attack right there." That will become important later.

But there was also Judge Grund, a man who besides being on the bench was serving as chairman of the Polk County draft board. Those things would seem to indicate he was well thought of by the public, but Babe portrays him—and Clark Mollenhoff concurs—as something of a money-grubbing numskull when it came to the law.

On January 12, 1946, Babe went to the Des Moines YMCA in his continuing effort to maintain his old fighter's physique while leading a nightclub life. He did a little workout and then ran into Judge Grund in the hallway. "I caught him out there, and he mentioned the two booze charges I had up against me," Babe said. "I said, 'Why do you guys have it in for me?' He said, 'You dagos want to run the whole town.'

"Well, I don't mind if I call myself a dago, or if some friend does in a nice way, but I wasn't going to take that from him. So I said, 'You sheeny son of a bitch,' and I grabbed him by the arm. Then we got away from each other."

The *Register*'s account of the incident said that "Bisignano shook him violently and accused him of taking money from people to keep them out of the army. Grund was chairman of the local draft board." Judge Grund went back to his court and stewed about the matter for a few days.

In Babe's current version of the story, he says he made a bad mistake. "What I did was call up the other judge, the one who was screwing my piano player," he said. "He started giving me some trouble about getting into that argument with Judge Grund, so I said, 'Well, you ain't pure, either. How long you been screwing my piano player up in my office? Maybe it's time I called your wife and told her about that.' I'd never do that kind of thing, but I thought I ought to scare him a little."

What that judge did, Babe says, "is to go to Judge Grund and tell him, and then Judge Grund said I'd have to learn the hard way. That's when he filed contempt of court charges against me for that shoving thing over at the YMCA." The case went to trial in Judge Grund's Municipal Court with Judge Grund, who you'll remember had filed the charges, hearing the case.without a jury.

The testimony was as interesting as you might expect. In one comment, the judge said, "As far as a personal attack on Harry Grund, that could be laughed off. No one was hurt. But this was an assault on the integrity of the court." In his sentencing remarks, he said, "I am not going to degrade the court or what the court stands for by telling Al Bisignano what kind of man he is."

Babe was, needless to say, found guilty. He appealed to the Iowa Supreme Court, which upheld the conviction. He appealed to the U.S. Supreme Court, which refused to hear the case, meaning the conviction would stand, and Babe entered 1947 knowing he was going to do a six-month jail sentence. "And I spent more than a hundred thousand dollars on that," he said.

A couple of other intriguing things happened in the course of it, too. One was, according to reporter Mollenhoff, that Judge Grund "got caught, literally, with his pants down." Besides being a judge, he also maintained a private law office in a building not far from the courthouse and not far from Babe's restaurant. There'd been talk, Mollenhoff said, about Judge Grund's eye for women.

He wound up getting caught with one in his private office. "It happened when she started screaming 'Rape! Rape!' out the window, and there just happened to be a couple of cops who were friends of Babe's on the street and they went running up the fire escape to save her and find Judge Grund," Mollenhoff said.

The woman also happened to be working as a waitress for Babe at the time. Babe only said of her, "There were always a lot of rumors about her."

The other thing that happened was that late on Christmas Eve of 1946, Des Moines police were called to the home of Polk County Attorney Vernon Seeburger because there was one very angry Babe Bisignano on his front porch. Seeburger told the officers and the media that Bisignano had been "hounding me for months" about booze charges pending against his restaurant and that Bisignano was specifically objecting to the county attorney's having obtained a court order that would padlock Babe's place for a long period of time.

"What really happened," said Babe in a story supported by later press stories and by other people in interviews, "was that Seeburger had been up for election that fall. I gave five thousand dollars to him, through a middleman, with the understanding that he'd take care of those booze charges against me. He got beat in the election, he hadn't done anything for me, and here we were down to the end of the year and he was going to be leaving office at the first of the new year.

"I got a little drunk that night, but the reason I went out there really was because I'd given that guy the money and he didn't do what he was supposed to do. I was just going out there to get my money back." The cops who answered the call, Babe said, "finally talked me into cooling down and leaving with them because it was Christmas Eve and all. They drove me around for a long time." Babe filed a civil lawsuit against the county attorney, seeking his money back, but the case was dismissed after an out-of-court settlement was reached between the two litigants.

Babe's six months in jail and the padlocking of his restaurant in 1947—an Alcoholics Anonymous chapter took the place over while he was gone and used it for their meetings—were among the most-covered events in Des Moines media history. Keep in mind that by then he was a man who was getting more press than the governor of Iowa, and here he was going to the calaboose.

In March of 1947, the *Tribune* reported that Babe, then suffering from ulcers while in jail, "daily receives a quart of goat's milk for his stomach ailment. He pays for it himself." The same story told of his immense popularity, both with his jailmates and with the concerned public:

> The some 100 prisoners in the county jail have profited from Bisignano's confinement, jail officers reported. The bulk of the weekly delivery of boxes and baskets of fruit, candy and tobacco from Bisignano's friends is divided up on Bisignano's direction for distribution to the other prisoners. Thursday, visiting day, about 60 persons visited Bisignano at the jail.

It was a time, obviously, of great stress on most of his family. But his daughter, Sister Judy, said, "I guess I was so young that they thought I couldn't understand, so they told me he was in a hospital, and even though I'd go down there and visit him, I never realized anything different than what I'd been told."

Babe's son Joe, who was older at the time, knew what was going on but isn't bitter about it. "I suppose I didn't really relate to what he'd done to be there," Joe said, "and the funny thing about it is that I actually have some of my fondest memories of close times with him when he was there. One morning a week, we'd all get out of school and go visit him as a family. And I'll never forget on Easter Sunday, they had a Mass at the jail and Dad and I were the altar boys for the priest."

The truth is, said Babe, it's something of a wonder all those visitors could even find him at the jail "because I wasn't really there a lot of the time. During the days, I was on what must have been the first work-release program, going out and doing things in the city, and I had this deal at night where—what the hell, I knew all of the guys around there—they'd let me out and I'd go spend the night at home until about four in the morning and then they'd sneak me back in.

"On that work-release thing, for a while they were sending me out to the county juvenile home and I was sort of a groundskeeper, working on the flower beds and all that. It was a nice time of the year, so I'd be wearing my wrestling trunks and trying to get a suntan while I was working. While I was out there, I found out that the juvenile home wasn't buying meat from my meat market I owned then, Casson's. So I sold them on buying from me.

"Then one day, I'm out there in the flower beds along the long driveway and in comes this Casson's truck, and the kid driving it was going way too fast. He damned near ran over me. He went on in and made his delivery, and I swore I'd get him on his way out. So he's leaving and I wave him down and stop him. I said, 'What the hell are you doing driving like that? You almost ran over me!' He looked at me and knew I was a prisoner and smarted off. He said what the hell difference did it make to me? I said, 'That's my truck and you work for me.'

"He thumbed his nose at me and went back to the plant. He went up to the manager and starts telling him about this crazy guy out at the juvenile home saying that he owned the truck and this business. The manager said, 'Well, that guy was right. He's the boss and we all work for him.' That was the end of that kid. I guess he didn't think there was much future for him in a corporation where the boss was working on a rockpile."

Babe said he ate few of his meals at the jail, and those that he did, "I'd have brought in." The other prisoners loved it, especially the "banquet" he threw on the night before he was released. Not only were the prisoners his guests, but so were all the jailers, and there's an outrageous picture of all of them grinning with their arms draped over each other's shoulders while standing and seated before a full table.

The nights away got a little bit tricky, he said, "because we had these two deputies who were the early-morning jailers, and they were the only two who didn't know what was going on. We were a little late coming back one morning, and we could see them through the window sitting in there and didn't know how we were going to sneak me by them.

"So the deputy who was driving me, I gave him a dime and I told him to go over to the pay phone that was there nearby and to call the jail and report that there was a big robbery in progress at this gambling joint out west of town and that people had been tied up and all that. He told those two guys that if they hurried, they could catch the guys there. So then we sat and watched them go running out of the jail with their shotguns, jump in a car, and take off. That's how I got back in that time."

But Babe will never forget one of the nights that he indeed did spend behind bars. "I was sitting there and they came and said there was a phone call for me," he said. "I picked it up and it was Frank Comfort, a dear guy who was my lawyer. He was more of a business lawyer than a criminal lawyer, and I think that's why I wound up in jail in the first place. He was also real big in politics in Iowa, and he also liked his Scotch.

"So he calls that night and he sounded a little drunk. He said, 'Babe, guess who I've got sitting right here in my home?' I said, 'Who?' He said, 'Tom Clark, the attorney general of the United States of America!'

"I said, 'Well, Frank, guess who you've got sitting down here in jail?' He said, 'Who?'

"I said, 'Me, you son of a bitch.'"

116

10

ON THE MATTER OF THE MAFIA

"You square guys, you don't know how it is."

OST OF THE PEOPLE who have come into Babe's restaurant over the decades have come in with at least some knowledge of all he's done in the past. You might think they come in in spite of what they know. But the truth is, more come *because* of it. They like a clean and decent place with good food, which it is and has. But they also like a place that has that certain feeling of being—although clearly safe now—a place where once upon a time the law was certainly bent, if not broken.

Does that make sense? It does to Babe himself. "That's an interesting thing," he said. "There is something about people that they seem to like it more if they feel like they're getting away with something."

The question up front in most of their minds, of course, is one that he says has only been directly asked of him twice: "Are you, or have you ever been, connected with the Mafia?"

The first time it was asked, he said, "was when some sweet little old lady who was in there asked me.

"I said, 'Ma'am, have you seen what I've been doing around here tonight? I've been going all over here with a towel over my arm and cleaning up dishes from the tables. The Mafia does not bus dishes.'"

The second time it was asked, he said, was when I did. "Aw, come on," he said. "That's ridiculous. What kind of question is that? You're just looking for something juicy to throw into this book. I'm more against the Mafia than you are. First of all, I'm of Italian descent, and we've all grown up knowing that any time the real Mafia did any of the stuff they did, we all get blamed for it. We get real tired of that.

"Yeah, I did some bootlegging. And yeah, I got some phony meat stamps back when it was being rationed in the war, but I was feeding ninety-five percent of that meat to service people.

"I've had my share of union troubles. I've had friends in Chicago. I've had some pretty scary things happen over the years. Jimmy Hoffa and lots of others have been in my place to eat. But me being in the Mafia, come on! What kind of question is that?"

Well, it's probably an ethnic slur of a question. But it ought to be pursued here, just the same.

So, point blank: Babe Bisignano, are you in the Mafia?
"No."
Were you ever?
"No."
Have you ever met a Mafia member?
"No. I've met some people who are probably considered gangsters, but the Cosa Nostra? No, no, no."

118

But there has always been public speculation, unjustified, that he could not get away with all he got away with, in the time he was getting away with it, without somehow being "connected." I mean, bribing cops, bribing the county attorney, buying booze when virtually no one else could get it, roughing people up. Yes, he was arrested a bundle of times and, yes, he did some jail time, but could he have gone on and survived if he hadn't at least made some kind of personal and business peace with the Mafia—which was controlling most of the nation's illegal activity and roughness at that time?

"No," he said again. "There's nothing to it."

I reminded him that in the middle of one of our interviews in his den, we were interrupted by a telephone call. He was talking to a lawyer in Mason City about a man who owed Babe money and who was dodging repayment. The lawyer apparently told Babe that the man was saying that there was no debt because they hadn't signed a contract.

"He says we didn't have a contract?" Babe said over the phone. "Well, you tell him I've got my own ways of getting contracts." Later, I asked him what he meant by that. Was he talking about a contract on the guy's life? Was Babe indicating he'd hire some hitmen to go do a number on this guy?

"Aw, come on," he said.

Well, then, what did he mean?

"I meant these," he said, holding up his own two fists.

You're seventy-five years old, I told him. How long do you think you can keep offering to fight somebody without getting really beat up yourself? How long are you going to go on fighting?

"All my life," he said. "I go by one rule: They can kill you but they can't eat you."

Yes, he said, he did some favors for some policemen. "But in those times, those guys are only making $175 a month or something like that," he said. "What's the matter with slipping them a ham or something like that?"

Yes, he tried to bribe the county attorney. "But I've told

you how that turned out—I didn't get nothing for it," he said.

"Hey, come on, there's nothing wrong with that stuff," he continued. "That's the American way of doing things. It's not what you know, it's who you know. You square guys, you don't know how it is. I go more by God's law than by the city, state, or federal laws."

He said most of the stories about him and the Mafia are the mind work of square guys who are "narrow-minded and are watching too much TV. There's this guy Gene Kennedy, a friend of mine from Dubuque, who used to be a legislator and is now a lobbyist, and a good one," he said. "One time he comes to me and he says he has proof that the Mafia is in Iowa, so I asked him what the proof was. He said his barber in Dubuque told him that he could make a bet and that the barber could make a call and get it placed. I said, 'Come on, Gene. What your barber is doing is calling a bookie! That ain't Mafia stuff!' "

There is, he said, "nothing for the Mafia to come here for." He repeated that he never knew a Mafioso.

But, wait. He did buy Canadian Ace beer, which was Mafia-controlled, and illegal booze from them, didn't he? And hasn't he frequently acted a little, uh, that way? You know, tough?

"Yeah, we bought it from them, truckloads of it," said Babe's brother, Chuck, who worked for Babe for a time and then started his own business. "But the truth is, we were never really connected to them. It was just a matter that they had the booze and no one else did, and we needed to buy it from them. We all did. It was just a business deal. They just sort of tolerated us. Look, Des Moines was a city of scarcely 140,000 people back then, and there just wasn't anything for them to really come in here for when they could do so much more in larger cities."

Chuck Bisignano can remember when one time, the feds "had all the highways shut down for booze shipments. That time, I was the only one in town who had any booze coming in. Not even Babe could get it. I had figured out how to have it shipped on Railway Express, and it was coming in labeled as 'olive oil' or some goddamn thing. Some of my best customers at that time were the judges and the attorneys who were right across the street in the courthouse from my joint."

And he can remember when a booze delivery was made personally by Ralph Capone, who was a brother of the most notorious Mafioso, Al Capone. "He came in driving a big Cord automobile and it was packed with booze," Chuck said. All of that was just a fact of business life for a tavern operator in that time, he said. Some flaunted their connections, some didn't. Chuck Bisignano says he didn't.

But he added, "There were times when Babe operated as if he was in the Mafia, even though he never was. But Babe had the guts, and he was big. He was tough and mean, and he could stand up to anybody. And I think he took advantage of that. People would feel like they were getting some kind of experience in it by coming into his place. It was more like Babe operated his own little Mafia in Des Moines."

Clark Mollenhoff, the reporter who watched Babe so closely in those years, agrees. "I think Babe was always one step removed from the actual mob," said Mollenhoff, who had plenty of experience covering all kinds of racketeering on the national scene. "He had his own local circles of influence, but I don't think it ever got beyond that."

Babe's circles of influence, and the way they were operated, are the stuff that would make polite company blush, if not quake. Mollenhoff himself was twice a victim, if you want to call it that. Now, in telling this, let me say that in their old age, Babe Bisignano and Clark Mollenhoff have patched up a lot of their war-years feuds.

Said Mollenhoff: "When I've been back in Des Moines in recent years, I've gone to Babe's and had dinner and talked to him, and it's been fine. I've discovered as I've gotten older that in a lot of cases, those people whom you were really combatants with earlier on become some of your most cherished acquaintances later on."

Babe is not quite as mellow. Mollenhoff, he said, remains the model he uses for his expression about reporters, about how they can be "just your typical newspaper prick." But where he used to say that Mollenhoff "should have died at birth," he now says, "Oh, maybe he should have been allowed to live for six months or so."

The basic problem is that Mollenhoff, who came out of Webster City to play football at Drake and become a young reporter for the *Register*, "kept going to all the officials" when Babe was pulling his stunts "and asking them what they were going to do about me," Babe said. Mollenhoff, I think, would accept that as true.

Babe thought that was an unnecessary intrusion into his life by a punk kid, even if Mollenhoff was so big and strapping that Babe once tried to hire him as a bouncer. So there came a time during the war when a service football team came into Des Moines to play Drake on a Saturday. But being a service team, the players were a little older and operated by looser rules than most college football players did. In other words, they came to town several days early and were hanging out at Babe's.

He got to know them and "I started telling them how much trouble this Drake player Clark Mollenhoff was giving me," Babe said. "So they said they could do something about that. Early in that game when the ball was snapped, eleven of them hit Mollenhoff all at once, and he was done for the day."

Another time, Mollenhoff said, he had written a story quoting a local official about how most of the nightclubs in the city were operating by the laws but that there were three that were causing problems, those owned by Babe, Johnny Critelli, and Al Rosenberg.

"So that story ran in the paper," Mollenhoff said, "and a day or so later, I was coming out of the courthouse on my way back to the paper and this big car pulled up. The three of them got out of the car and told me to get into it, that we were going to go for a little ride. I was a little bit scared, but at the same time, I was a college football player, and I told myself that if it got too bad, I could surely outrun them after I got a few licks in of my own.

"We drove around for a while, and I was telling them, 'Look, I didn't say you had bad places. I was just quoting that official saying you had problems.' That's when Babe said, 'Well, how can that guy say that after all the money I've given him?' And the other two chipped in and said they'd given him money, too. We went to the back room of Critelli's place and kept talking, and they all told me they would talk on the record about how they'd bribed this guy.

"So I got that story, which was my first story about a payoff of a public official. The three of them not only gave me the story, they also drove me back to the paper and walked in and swore to Herb Kelly, my editor, that what I was writing was all true."

Babe recalled getting rough with various "tinhorn gangsters" he encountered over the years, too. "One night, this thief from Sioux City came in, a great big guy," Babe said. "He said he wanted five thousand dollars from me. I said, 'For what?' Hell, I thought he might be asking for a loan. He said, 'Because you might need me sometime.' I said, 'What the hell would I need you for? Are you trying to muscle me?' Then I grabbed him and I threw him down the stairs."

But another time, the threat was more serious. That was when Babe owned Casson's meat market, and a thug came in from Detroit to try to organize the workers into a union.

"He was telling them all kinds of stuff," Babe said. "He said they shouldn't worry about me because, 'In Detroit, we know how to handle those dagos—we just put them in cement and throw them into the river.' So one night, I start doing some drinking. I hit several joints. I get to one, and the waitress gets worried and she calls my friend Lou Farrell and tells him that she's never seen me drink this way and that he should come and get me." Lou Farrell, it should be noted, is the Americanized name of Luigi Fratto, who came to Des Moines from Chicago with a tale that he was indeed a Mafioso. "He hurt himself that way," said Babe. "I never knew of anything he did wrong, but he wanted to make people think that way."

At any rate, Farrell showed up at a local lounge to retrieve his friend Babe, but instead the two wound up drinking together, and before the night was over, they went to the Savery Hotel to confront the union organizer.

"We got him in his room up on the eighth floor," said Babe. "We roughed him up a little and we leaned him out on the windowsill, like we were going to throw him out. We weren't going to do that, of course, but he thought we were. So he took off running and ran down eight flights of stairs. I heard later the guy slept in the boiler room all that night."

Luigi Fratto, or Lou Farrell, was a lot of talk, Babe said. Fred Eckrosh, Babe's longtime and frank-talking friend, agrees with that. "Lou came into Des Moines talking about how the Mafia had sent him in here from Chicago," Eckrosh said. "If that was true, it must have been a matter of him screwing up so bad in Chicago that they sent him to Des Moines to get him out of town. He was always a lot of big talk, but whenever it came to getting anything done, I never knew of him being able to do it."

Babe has run in rough company over the years and says, "One fear I always had was that I might be kidnapped—not in any Mafia-type thing but by somebody who thought I'd be worth a lot of money. The truth is I never carry much money, and I've thought sometimes I should always have a few hundred on me because if somebody kidnapped me and I only had a few bucks, they might think I was holding out on them. One time for fun, I asked Katy how much ransom she'd be willing to pay if I did get kidnapped, and she said, 'If they wanted more than five hundred dollars, they could keep you.' "

Within the last decade, he said, he was called to come to the Des Moines Police Station where detectives played him a tape recording of a phone call in which somebody was saying "there was somebody coming in to knock me off." The call was investigated, Babe said, but turned out to be a crank.

He's thought enough about it, however, that he does maintain some personal protection. "I don't have a gun, I'd be afraid I'd wake up in the middle of the night and be confused and shoot myself," he said. "But I do keep a ball bat around."

That doesn't sound like much of a Mafioso to me.

11

MEETING HIS FATHER AGAIN

". . .I didn't even fee

ke he was my dad."

HAVING DELVED this deeply into his life, some of you have probably concluded that Babe Bisignano is a bad man.

There is an abundance of evidence to the opposite, and no piece of that evidence is more impressive than what Babe tried to do for his father late in the father's life.

It didn't work. The old scoundrel, Genaro "George" Bisignano, remained as bad in his eighties as he'd been thirty years earlier when he abandoned his family, never sent any word about where he was, never sent a dime of support, and never displayed an ounce of concern. "That bastard," as his daughter Dee Kelleher has already called him here, was a bastard to the end. And because his efforts turned out that way, it could be a key to why it's hard for Babe Bisignano, burned so many times in his life, to consider a reconciliation in the sad relationship with his own children today.

"It was in the late 1950s sometime, and this truck driver came into my restaurant and told one of my people that he wanted to see me," Babe said. "He was dressed bad, and I thought he was probably some guy going to try to hit me up for a couple of hundred bucks to go on his trip or something.

"But the guy said, 'I'm from Chicago, and I know quite a bit about you. I know your dad.' The first thing I said was, 'Is he alive?' He said, 'Yeah, he's running a little restaurant on skid row in Chicago. He feels real bad about what happened, and he isn't doing too good now. He's getting sick.' The truck driver gave me the address in Chicago, but no way was I going to rush out there. After all those years without ever hearing from him, I didn't even feel like he was my dad.''

But six months later, business took Babe and two friends from Des Moines to Chicago, where they purchased some new restaurant equipment. "We got done, and I thought, 'What the hell,' so we went down and found that address," he said. "It was a little greasy spoon, a few stools at a counter and a few tables. We walked in, and I saw him right away. He was a lot grayer and he was wearing glasses, but I recognized him. He said, 'Hi, boys, what can I get you?' I said, 'You remember me?' He still had that Italian accent and he said, 'Well, your face-a look-a familiar, but I forgot-a your name.'

"I said, 'That's too goddamn bad about you that you can't remember me. I happen to be your son Alphonse.' I thought he was going to have a stroke or something. He sat down at a table and put his head in his hands. It was so sad that the other two guys with me walked out. I put my hand on his shoulder and said, 'Well, Pa, don't you want to ask about Grandma and the other kids?'

"He said, 'Please, leave-a me alone. Leave-a me alone. I'm-a nervous. I'm-a nervous.' I was still smoking then, so I waited for a few minutes and said, 'Do you sell cigarettes?' He said, 'They got-a them next door in the little tavern, but how long-a you been-a smoking?' So he went next door with me, and I bought some drinks for everybody in there. Then when I ordered a second drink for myself, he said to me, 'You drink-a too much.' Here he was correcting me already. He thought I was fifteen years old or something. He'd been gone for thirty years, and he's correcting me.''

Babe said, "I tried to talk him into giving the keys to his restaurant to a cop and coming back home to Des Moines with me, but he wouldn't do it—he said he had five hundred dollars tied up in it. So I finally left and tried to forget about it."

It was about a year later, Babe said, "when one night we were packed at the restaurant, I mean really packed. I was upstairs in the supper club, and I got word that he'd walked in downstairs and that he'd already propositioned two or three of my waitresses. I went running right down there, and the first thing he did was start giving me hell for having too many employees. It was awful. That time, he hung around Des Moines for about a week, and then he went back to Chicago and we didn't hear anything else from him for more than a year."

Then one day, Babe said, "I got a call from a flophouse in Chicago, and this guy said, 'Your dad wanted me to call you. He's pretty sick and he might not make it.' I've got a cousin in Chicago, so I called him and asked him to go over, check it out, and if he was really sick to get him to the best Catholic hospital in Chicago, give them my name and bank references, and take care of him.

"So that's what happened. Then a doctor called me one day and said, 'Mr. Bisignano, I've done about all I can for your father. He's just old and worn out, and he should be put in a nursing home.' So I called my cousin again and told him to go get him and put him on a train to Des Moines and I'd get him taken care of.

"I'll never forget going down to the Rock Island train station. I had my brother Chuck with me. Dad got off that train, and he was carrying a suitcase tied together with a rope. I said, 'There he is, Chuck. Go get him.' I'll tell you, Katy and I didn't even want to see him and neither did my sisters."

Chuck Bisignano, who'd been so young when he'd last seen his father, was not surprised when the old man didn't recognize him. "I had no bitterness about it," Chuck said, "because if I'm bitter about something, I'm not feeling good. I don't know, he must have had an awful tough life himself. And maybe what he did to us had made us all better people."

Babe had arranged for a private room for his father at the Bishop Drumm Catholic nursing home in Des Moines. That's where they took him. "I'll never forget going in there with him," Babe said. "First of all, he was mad because he said it was a place 'for old people.' He wanted to stay at my house, and I said, 'No way.' But there we have him in his room, and he starts to open his suitcase. A whole bunch of dirty underwear and the worst pornography I've ever seen fell out. Awful pictures. And it was right in front of a nun. I was so embarrassed I was about to die. I said, 'Sister, I'm really sorry for this,' but she said, 'Well, Babe, we're used to dealing with a lot here.'"

Amazingly, after a time, Genaro Bisignano started feeling better, to the point where he would come downtown to Babe's restaurant a couple of times a week. "He'd come in at noon and look at my buffet lines, which were real busy, and he started telling me he thought I should let him take that over to run it, that I owed him that," Babe said.

"Then one day, he just disappeared from the Bishop Drumm home. I figured he'd just gone back to Chicago. But a week or two later, I get a call from some character who's running this low-rent apartment place here in Des Moines, and he said, 'If you're such a big shot, why don't you come up here and pay your father's rent?' I went up and paid it.

"Then Dad kept coming downtown and wanting a piece of my restaurant. He finally said if I didn't let him have some of it, he'd open a place of his own 'and disgrace me.' I asked him if he didn't think he'd caused me enough grief already.

"But he went out and got this place over on the east side, a little bit of a place across the tracks. It looked a lot like the place he'd had in Chicago. He put up a big sign out in front that said 'Bisignano's.' Then he went around to the restaurant supply places. He's going in there telling them he's my father, and since I'm doing so much business with them, they're giving him everything he needs to open.

"He did open it. But he was at least eighty years old by then and sick, and the place didn't last long. He died before long, but the hell of it was that then I found out he'd left all these markers out there with these supply places, so I had to go around and cover them."

The surviving members of Genaro Bisignano's family—Babe, Chuck, and their sister Dee Kelleher—all went to his funeral and burial in Des Moines in 1961. But, you know, all three said they can barely remember anything about it.

Little wonder.

12

HE KNOWS EVERYBODY

" 'We got a Big Ma
a Big Man fror

ith us today,
owntown.' "

BECAUSE of Babe Bisignano's big restaurant operation, his big wallet, his big personality, and his big heart, he has come to know personally more of the high and mighty, as well as the low and power-less, than most of us ever will.

"Look, I don't consider myself famous," he said. "But after fifty years in the limelight, I know I'm a character. I know I'm colorful. Way back there, I wrestled in Yankee Sta-dium and I wrestled in Madison Square Garden. I was a show-man then, and I'm a showman now. That's let me meet a lot of people, and it's nice to be recognized. But the little people have always known that I'm just like them."

He's been to the White House. (That was in 1980 at a reception President Jimmy Carter put on for his Iowa sup-porters. Babe wore a tuxedo for the first time in his life and, according to his friend Jim Rasley, stole a piece of silverware and then later was reprimanded by the Secret Service for attempting to pee in the bushes.) He's also been to the poor-house. To his credit, he recognizes there are basically good people in both of them, some needing more help than others, and some helpless and hopeless.

Let's listen to him talk about them.

John Ruan and Bill Knapp, two of the reigning business and social tycoons in Des Moines: "Oh, those guys are all right. I can go the same places they can, I just can't stay as long. You know what the difference between those two guys is? John Ruan doesn't know who the police chief of Des Moines is at any particular time, and Bill Knapp always wants to appoint the police chief. But I like that Knapp. One time there was this big building project being talked about for downtown Des Moines, and part of it was going to be that the city would have to condemn my restaurant so they could get the land. Bill Knapp was quoted in the paper saying, 'It'd be easier to condemn the state capitol than it would be to condemn Babe's restaurant.' I liked that."

There's the cook who stole his Oldsmobile 98 station wagon: "This guy had gone to work for me, and he seemed like a great guy." He was real active in his church, and all that. He was so religious that he finally told me that if the swearing didn't stop at my place, he was quitting. I liked him, so then he comes up and said he wanted to go to California to see his sister but he didn't have any way out there. So I go get new tires and get the car all tuned up, and I let him use it to go out there. That was two years ago, and I haven't had any contact from him since."

Lute Olson, the former University of Iowa basketball coach now at the University of Arizona: "The phoniest guy I ever met. Big crybaby."

Tom Abatemarco, the new Drake University basketball coach: "You can have him. He's a big loud-mouthed Italian. He doesn't know when to shut up." But then, in perhaps a takes-one-to-know-one mood, "Oh, I think we'll eventually get along."

134

Terry Branstad, the governor of Iowa: "Not a bad little guy. He's not colorful. I kind of feel sorry for him."

Willie Thomas (who?): "Willie Thomas was one of the best guys I've ever met. I suppose it was six or seven years ago. He worked for me as a busboy at noon, and he was an old man, maybe eighty. Great guy. He was real religious, and sometimes we'd be missing him at noon. I'd go down in the basement and find him down there reading the Bible. I finally had to stop that by telling him, 'Willie, there is God's time and there is Babe's time.' But I really liked that man—he was a good one—and all my customers and workers loved him.

"Willie died, and they had his funeral over at this black church in Des Moines, and there was no way I was going to miss it. I went over there, and it was hot—God was it hot! People were fainting right and left, and there were these ladies all dressed in white who were going around fanning everybody. I'm sitting there, thinking about Willie and feeling sad and all of a sudden I hear the minister saying, 'We got a Big Man with us today, a Big Man from downtown. He loved Willie, and Willie loved him. Babe, would you like to say something?' I didn't know that was coming, and I was shook. I don't know how I ever got up there, but I did.

"I told those people about how much I liked Willie. Then I looked down at his coffin there and I said, 'You know, if I could trade places with Willie right now, I think I would, because we all know where Willie is—in heaven—and I'm not so sure where I'm going.'

"So I got done, and I sat down. And then the minister said, 'It takes a Big Man to say what Babe just said! It takes a Big Man to say he doesn't know where he's going! How many of you know where you're going?' He went on and on about that. I'll tell you, by the time it was over, I walked out of there as limp as a dishrag. And I was wanting to say my own thing to God, that 'God, I didn't really mean that I wanted to change places with Willie right this minute.' "

135

Let's move on to what people say about Babe.

There are the ladies of "Babe's Babes" bowling team. He's sponsored them in Des Moines bowling competition for forty-eight consecutive years. They used to be all blondes and were known as "Babe's Blondes," but as age has come upon them, they've changed the name. "We check in with him every so often," said team member Melba King. "He's told us he guessed he'd be our sponsor as long as we can walk—and some of us are able to do that, barely. But fun we do have."

United States Senator Dennis DeConcini, the Arizona Democrat—Babe met him through his daughter Sister Judy, who runs the school in Tucson that DeConcini's children have all attended. DeConcini and his family, Babe said, have probably given more money to Sister Judy's school than he has. "You know, Babe once gave me one thousand dollars for a campaign, and I doubt he's contributed to a lot of other political campaigns," DeConcini said. "I was flattered.

"I think what I like about him is the thing I like about my father. Both have a lot of money, but they're frugal and they don't waste it. Babe comes from that old school—an immigrant's child who's done well and remembers how hard it was to do it. Those who were ethnic hard workers are the ones who've made entrepreneurship in this country what it is today. Those people succeeded without having a lot of education, and that's become more impressive to those of us in this era when almost everybody has to have a college education to succeed. How did they do it?"

As with Senator DeConcini and with Sister Judy's school, Babe has given, given, and given some more, if you want to talk money. But more impressive than political contributions or other ultimately tax-deductible gifts is the money he's handed out in one- and five- and twenty-dollar

136

bills, sometimes even more, to the destitute in Des Moines. When I asked him what it would amount to over his career, he thought for a long time and said, "a hundred thousand dollars—conservatively." Why does he do that?

"Because I was so poor myself when I grew up," he started. "I mean really poor. I can remember so well when streetcar tickets were two for a nickel and, hell, I was still walking.

"So then I go on and I start making some money myself. And being on a main street downtown, you see a lot of people who need help. Hell's fire, if some wino comes to me and he wants a buck or two to get another bottle, I never expect to get that back. What the hell, another bottle of wine isn't going to change his life.

"Yeah, you do get hit by some con artists. Some guy stops in and says his car's broken down on the highway and he needs fifty dollars. That might be honest and it might not be. You get burned sometimes and you get bitter and you say you'll never give anybody another dime. But then you turn around and do. "It's just your nature. Either you help people or you don't. A lot of people helped me way back there."

Of course, by his own admission, Babe now has it to give. He is, he said, a regular bettor on college sports, although now he is "just a hundred-dollar bettor," which is a far cry from a few years ago.

And then there's golf. He's played in some of the top pro-am tournaments in America—the Andy Williams, the Joe Garagiola, and others—on some of the most exotic courses there are.

"I used to be able to shoot in the mid- to upper seventies," he said. "But then my back started giving me problems, and I'm lucky now if I can break 100. But I'll tell you one thing, I never have trouble getting games. If I lose, my money is up front. There are no IOUs."

137

Sometimes, it comes his way. Johnny Orr, the Iowa State University basketball coach, has played in the Babe/Mercy Hospital Golf Classic, to which Babe annually lends his name to help raise money for the Des Moines hospital's alcohol and drug rehabilitation programs.

"I suppose it's been two or three years ago now," Orr said. "My group followed his group, and he was playing awful. He couldn't make anything. I'd watch him on the greens, and he couldn't even drop a two-foot putt. So we get up to this one hole behind them, and he's got about a ten-footer. I said, 'If you make that, I'll write a personal check for a hundred dollars to the hospital.' Damned if he didn't. I wrote him the check."

Sometimes, the money flows the other way on the links. For years, Babe was a regular in a money game in which Floren DiPaglia, a Des Moines businessman who's had his share of legal problems, was a participant. Babe said their wagers sometimes amounted to four thousand dollars per hole.

As Babe tells the story: "See, there was this game and I was playing against DiPaglia. Well, DiPaglia ain't no altar boy, as they say, and I always believe that when in Rome, do as the Romans. So he hits this shot into a deep rough, and we're over there looking for it, knowing if he can't find it, it'll cost him a stroke. DiPaglia gets kind of off to himself, and the next thing we know is he's yelling that he found it.

"I says, 'How could you have found it? I got it right here in my pocket!' "

DiPaglia confirmed that story, with one refinement. "Yeah," said the sixty-two-year-old-who has been working in building supplies. "No question about it. There were some big money games. I remember beating him out of thirteen thousand dollars one day, probably in about 1951. But then a second day, we played again, and Babe and his partner got me and my partner for fifteen thousand dollars."

The refinement he made was that "on that same hole where he had my ball in his pocket, which really happened, well, he'd hit a bad shot, too, and couldn't find it. The truth is I found his ball and had it in my own pocket."

Sports—of any kind—have always been big to Babe Bisignano, and they've been big business, too. Most all teams and coaches who visit Des Moines eat and drink at his restaurant. "Funny how they all seem to start at my place, isn't it?" he said.

He reciprocates, too. When those television "rasslin' " stars of the modern day came to Des Moines two years ago, one in their number was observing a birthday. They all showed up at Babe's to celebrate, and he was at the height of his glory. He and Hulk Hogan, the blond behemoth who is the most famous of them all, posed for a photo, which Babe now reproduces by the hundreds. He autographs them and gives them away to kids, always signing, "I'm the one on the left."

When the late coach Maury John had a good basketball team at Drake, Babe was a big booster. And although a bettor, he also tells this story: "One time, one of the kids who was a star on that team came to me and said, 'What's the line you're getting on our next game?' I told that kid, 'Listen, don't you ever say something like that to me or anybody else again.' Then I called Maury and told him about it. I don't mind betting, but I hate that stuff about players fixing games."

Another Drake team had a good season but was denied a berth in the National Invitational Tournament at Madison Square Garden in New York City despite the fact that several teams Drake had beaten were invited. Babe jumped on an airplane and went to the Big Apple. He picketed under the Garden's marquee, carrying a sign that told the scores by which Drake had beaten the qualifying teams. His photo was snapped doing that, and Babe again made the national news.

Babe was especially attached to an earlier Drake basketball coach, John Bennington, who left Des Moines to coach at the University of St. Louis and at Michigan State before his death. "I'll never forget one winter night when Bennington's Michigan State team was going to be playing at Minnesota," Babe said. "I called three other guys in Des Moines, and we all decided to go up to Minneapolis for that game.

"So we drove up there, and we went to the hotel where the Michigan State team was staying. We were around there having a few drinks, and when we saw John, he asked me how many tickets we needed and I said four. He gave me five, and said we might end up needing another one." (Now, if you believe the rest of this particular story, you must also believe that there is a huge naivete in Babe Bisignano. I *do* believe that, having seen it firsthand, like not knowing the difference between a "salon" and a "saloon.")

Before Bennington left the hotel with his team, he asked Babe to do him a favor. "I'm worried about the officiating tonight," the coach said, according to Babe. "The guy's name is Homer. You're going to be sitting right behind our bench, so would you yell 'Homer' a few times so that this official might give us a break?" Babe promised he would.

He and his three traveling companions found their seats behind the Michigan State bench in Williams Arena in Minneapolis and started watching the game. At the first opportunity, Babe yelled "Homer" so that the official could hear him. The official, whose name was *not* Homer, glared right back at him, because "homer" is what fans yell to accuse a referee of favoring the home team.

"I kept it up," Babe said. "The official came over to the Michigan State bench and said to John Bennington, 'You better shut up that loud-mouthed friend of yours, or I'm going to have him thrown out of here.' Bennington stood up and yelled right back at the official, 'What are you talking about? I don't even know that guy!' The next time down the floor, I yelled 'Homer' again, and the ref stopped the game.

"He called the cops in, and I mean to tell you, they picked me up and carried me all the way out of the auditorium without my feet ever touching the ground. What was really funny about it was that as they're jerking me out of there, John Bennington stood beside his bench, watching it all and smiling. As they were hauling me away, he waved and yelled, 'Don't forget—I gave you an extra ticket!' " Babe used the extra ticket, got back into the arena and watched the rest of the game in silence.

In case you think this craziness is restricted only to sports, hear now the story of the stained glass windows, from seven or eight years ago.

Babe is a sporadically avid antique collector. His collection is extensive and expensive. But surely no piece he holds has wound up being as costly as the stained glass windows that he *doesn't* have.

"I seen this ad in a newspaper," he said, "that the old Elks Club in Council Bluffs was being torn down and they had eight eight-foot by four-foot stained glass windows in the auction. So I went over and bought them and had them stored.

"I'd paid a good bit of money for them, even though I felt like I bought them right. I wanted to get them over to Des Moines, so one day, I said to my dear friend [the late] Max Holmes, Sr., that I needed to borrow a truck to go to Council Bluffs and pick them up. He said he could get the truck and he'd just go with me. So he came in this brand new pickup. I'd gone out and found some of those cushioned blankets that we could pack the windows in.

"We drove over to Council Bluffs, packed up the windows in the back of the truck, and then we stopped for dinner and a couple of drinks. We started back for Des Moines on Interstate 80, and this was when I was still smoking. Since it was a brand new truck, I didn't want to dirty up the ashtray, so I've got the little wing window open and I'm flicking my ashes and cigarettes out there. So we're driving along, and all of a sudden this big semi comes up alongside us and is flashing its spotlight at us and honking its horn. We pulled over and noticed that the load of stained glass windows was smoking. One of my cigarettes had blown back there and started it all on fire.

"The truck driver stopped, too, and came running over with a fire extinguisher. He sprayed the whole rear end of our truck. It was snowing real bad that night, so just to be sure, Max and I got out there alongside the road and made up a great, big snowball—we could hardly lift it—and we got it up there in the back of the truck just in case it started burning again.

"It did. We weren't a whole lot further down the interstate when another trucker did about the same thing—stopped us again. That stuff was smoldering again. That time, we got out there and, when we finally got it stopped, we took off some of those packing blankets I had those windows in and the leaded glass had all melted! The windows were just frames with all of that melted stuff on the bed of the truck. They were ruined!"

So what did two of the most prominent businessmen in Des Moines do at that point?

"We drove on to one of those rest stops along the interstate," said Babe. "We stopped there and we just pulled all that stuff out of the truck and left it as a big pile of junk beside the road."

Ah, Babe.

But it doesn't stop there. Let us now go to the fall of 1986, to Babe's chronic bad back, to his driver's license problems, and to his pal, Des Moines clothier Bill Reichardt.

"I hadn't seen him for quite some time," Reichardt said, "and then one day this lady from Dubuque who knows him came into my store. She said she'd checked on Babe while she was in town and that his back was so bad that he'd been at home in bed for several days.

"So I called him and said I was going to be over to pick him up and that we were going to go to my chiropractor to get him fixed up. He raised hell at first, but I said, 'Well, you can either stay there on your ass feeling sorry for yourself, or we can go get you back on your feet.' So he said to come get him.

"I went and got him and we were on our way to the chiropractor. He said he was sure glad I was driving because his driver's license had expired. I thought that was terrible, but then I looked at my own driver's license, and it had expired, too. So I told him that as soon as the chiropractor was done with him, we were going right over to the driver's license station and take the tests to renew. That's what we did.

"After twenty minutes, I was all done, handed it in, and I passed," Reichardt continued. "The reason I knew all that stuff was because I'd recently been through two speeder classes and I knew that state driver's manual real well. Then I went back to check on Babe. He was only on about the sixth question of about forty, and I corrected a couple of his answers. The lady who was running the place saw that and she said, 'Sir, you can't help him or I'll have to ask you both to leave.'"

Babe asked where the toilet was located and motioned Reichardt in with him.

"What he told me in there was that there was no way he could pass that test," Reichardt said.

Babe went back out and tried but indeed failed. "I had to bring him back out the next morning," Reichardt said. "This time, I stood right over the top of him. It's a multiple choice type of test, so when he was on any certain question, I'd tap him on the shoulder the number of times to correspond to whether the answer was 1, 2, 3, or 4. The lady caught us again.

"So I said, 'Ma'am, if I don't help this guy, I'm going to have to be bringing him back out here every morning for the rest of my life and the rest of yours because he's never going to pass any other way.'

143

"She looked at us and then she came over and said she would sit down with him and read him the questions. She was on one side of him and I was on the other, and I'm still tapping him the answers to the questions. He passed, and with a good score. And when he did, he was so thrilled that he grabbed that woman, twirled her around, and did a little dance with her. He said, 'I want you to come down to the restaurant. Bring your ma, bring your grandma, bring your kids—all on me.' "

When I ran Reichardt's story by Babe Bisignano, he smiled and then said it was all true. And then Babe, who drives every day, said, "And you know what? My driver's license has run out again. I don't have one right now."

When I raised hell, citing the possibilities of what he might lose if he was involved in an accident with no driver's license, he said, "Well, I know I've got to go renew it. And I know if I don't do it before this book comes out, I'm screwed."

It scared me. I'm not sure it scared him enough. But then, if there's anybody in Iowa who's accustomed to living on life's edge, it's Babe Bisignano.

ON HIS ETHNICITY

" 'It's us Italians against the rest of the world.' "

WHAT WE'RE TALKING right here is Italianness.

"My *compa*," Babe says, when talking about any of his tightest pals, although the way he says it, it sounds more like, "My *cumba*." That comes from the Italian word *compare*, which translates roughly as best friend, best man, or best buddy.

"It's the person who stands up with you when you get married, or the guy that's the godfather when your kids get baptized," Babe said. "It's somebody you can always go to for help."

"It's almost a spiritual sort of relationship," said John Pascuzzi, a Des Moines television personality who is also Italian. "In our modern way of speaking, it could be almost the same as when one guy refers to his friend as 'cuz' or something like that. It just reflects that natural bonding that exists between Italians."

Babe Bisignano has known about that forever, or at least since the first time he wrestled in Des Moines as a professional, attracting most of the south side for his match at the Coliseum with the renowned champion Earl Wampler, who was cast in the roll of the villain against the hometown kid.

Babe's memory is that Wampler kept telling him during the match that he could not only whip Babe, but all of his "dago and wop" friends in the audience, too. Wampler did indeed whip Babe, winding it up by getting an illegal vial of rubbing alcohol from his shorts and putting it in Babe's eyes and then kicking him in the groin before body-slamming him on the mat in front of the perplexed fans. Babe's last recollection of that fight is a bunch of south siders, including his little brother Chuck, filling the ring for a good ol' rasslin' riot.

Yes, Babe has always recognized the reality of *compas.* In fact, he thinks that one of the reasons his father left his family and Des Moines so many years ago is that "he may have owed some money to his *compas* and realized he couldn't repay it, and he was ashamed. I don't know that for sure, but I've always wondered if that wasn't the case."

Babe has plenty of his own *compas.* One certainly would be Carl Cacciatore, the boyhood chum who's remained a lifelong friend, despite some of the things Babe did to him early on. Like what?

"Carl was always one of the littler kids," Babe said, "and since I was one of the bigger ones, I ran some protection on him. When he was doing his paper route, I'd protect him from getting picked on for fifteen cents a week. Then one time I decided I ought to get twenty-five cents a week out of him, but he wouldn't pay it. I sent Ralph Costanzo out and had him rough up Carl a little bit—not hurt him, just rough him up. And then Carl decided the twenty-five cents was worth it."

But not all Babe's *compas* have been Italian. He made the late Dr. Eddie Anderson, long-ago coach of the University of Iowa Hawkeye football team, a *compa* by having him serve as godfather for Babe's daughter Mary Kay. Babe called him

146

and explained that being a godfather and thus becoming a *compa* meant, "I can call you up anytime from now on and get money from you if I need it."

The coach's response: "That works two ways, doesn't it?"

Bisignano, partly because of his celebrity, has become the most famous or at least most readily identifiable Italian in Iowa. There was the letter a couple of years ago from the third-grade teacher in Creston in southwest Iowa, saying that her class was studying Italy and there were no Italian people around for them to talk to. She wondered if Babe might come give a program on his ethnicity for her class. He did better than that. He brought them all to Des Moines for a pizza party at his restaurant and then regaled them with stories about his background.

But how much of what this guy is—and isn't—can be explained by his Italianness?

There is a lot more that gets all wound up in this—Catholicism, toughness, self-pity, a tendency to live outside the law, hard-headedness, totalitarianism in family relationships, ego, generosity, open passion but reserved emotion, self-deprecating humor. Let's look at some examples from the past.

On Catholicism: "I will never forget an airplane trip we were taking to visit a military base out in California," said Luther Glanton, a semiretired Polk County District Court Judge in Des Moines. "We had some wing trouble with the airplane. They tried to fix it, and then we left. But there was more trouble when we were in the air. The plane started shaking and it didn't look good. I was sitting right next to Babe, and I'll never forget how he pulled out those Rosary beads and started praying. He had us all saying the Rosary with him—even me, and I was a Baptist at the time."

On ego: Babe says to this day that he is sticking by his earlier pledge that none of the pallbearers at his own funeral will be from Des Moines "because I've got so many friends here that I don't want to pick six of them and have the rest feel slighted."

On toughness: There was the tiff that happened soon after Babe opened in 1939 with one of those would-be union organizers. An outside guy had come to Des Moines and was trying to organize the bartenders. Babe's bartender told Babe. Babe, of course, showed up at the meeting, coming in behind "this guy who had his feet on the table and his back to me. I jumped on him like a big bear. I rolled him all over the floor, banging him with lefts and rights. When they separated us, all he was complaining about was how I'd ripped up his shirt. So I went to the phone and called a friend of mine who ran a clothing store, and I asked him to come down to get this guy a new shirt. I wound up buying him a whole new suit, and the last thing I told him was that they usually bury a guy in a new suit—now all he needed was the coffin to go with it. I don't want people to think I'm a tough guy and shove people around but you can't have people pushing you around and hitting you up for money all the time."

On totalitarianism in family relationships: He learned it from *his* father. He recalls riding home from his mother's funeral in the car with his brothers and sisters, his father, and a good-hearted neighbor, Mrs. Keaney, who had seen to it that the children had enough to eat during the mother's illness. "Dad and Mrs. Keaney argued all the way," he said. "Dad made it plain to her that she was not to mingle in his home. He didn't want her ever to set foot in it. He told her he was now in complete charge of the family and that he would blow up her house if she stuck her nose into our affairs." As brother Chuck has said, that's just the way Italian fathers were then.

148

On the tendency to live outside the law: "I've always told my daughter, Sister Judy, who's always looking for money for this or that, that when she's really in trouble some place, the best thing she can do is to find out who the local bookie or bootlegger is and go to him," Babe said. "Those are people like me, the kind who'll help somebody who needs help. Professional people will help, too, but it takes them so much more time to decide to do it."

He's always been willing to fight when someone has slighted him for being Italian. From one of his own attempted manuscripts, he recalls a run-in when he was courting Catherine, who was running the candy shop.

"Catherine had a lady working for her by the name of Helen Fisher," Babe wrote. "Her husband was going around saying he couldn't understand why Catherine was going with a dago, and a wrestler at that. After hearing this in a couple of spots, I started looking for him. I heard he hung out at the Mission Pool Hall. It was on the second floor. Sure enough, there he was. He was sitting on a chair watching a billiard game. I was really mad, and before he got a chance to get out of the chair, I picked him and the chair up and slammed him to the floor. I was on top of him and going to give him a good going over. There were two detectives playing pool in the back of the house, and they came running out to break it up. They told us to get out, and if we caused any more trouble we would wind up in the can.

"We both started to leave, and just before he got to the top of the stairway, this guy, Fisher, went for a pool cue that was in a cue rack. He came towards me. I grabbed the cue and worked him over with it. The detectives came running again. One was an Irishman named Fitzpatrick. He said, 'All right, you guys, you're going to jail.' In those days, they [the detectives] had a big touring car with the top down. They put him in the front seat and me in the back seat. There was a policeman sitting with me in the back seat.

"The jail was just across the river. About the time we were on the bridge about a block from the jail, I started whacking him again and there we were fighting in this car. I pulled him back, and he landed on the floorboards with me on top of him. Fitzpatrick was on top of me trying to break it up. While they were booking us, this guy, Fisher, told the police, 'Whatever you do, don't put us in the same cell.'

"I was in the slammer about four hours. I was worried what Catherine would say. She acted like she was upset about the whole thing, but really, in her heart I think she understood how I felt."

Is all this Italianness? Or is this just a man of strong personality who is a product of his rough-and-tumble times?

There is no consensus.

His daughter, Sister Judy, has talked about how her father's Italianness is a real factor in his life, sometimes glorious and sometimes not.

Vic Gallo sees it the same way. Gallo is a sixty-eight-year-old keen "Babe watcher" from the northeast Iowa town of Oelwein, the home of many Italian families, including Gallo's. He met Bisignano when, as a young newspaperman in Strawberry Point, he came to Des Moines for a basketball tournament and ate and drank with Babe at the restaurant. Gallo later lived in Des Moines for a time, serving as state superintendent of printing, and became closer yet to Babe. In 1987, he wrote an original play, "Babe—The Life and Times of an Iowa Legend," which a theatrical troupe known as "The Big Ballroom Players" performed for sell-out crowds in Oelwein for two nights.

Gallo has studied Bisignano closely for a long time. "He's difficult to figure out, and yet he's not difficult at all to figure out," Gallo said. "He is a man of contrasting moods. One minute, he's the greatest guy in the world. The next, he's the most stubborn SOB there ever was.

"I definitely think his Italianness comes into play in what he is all about. I'm really from the same era that he is, and when we grew up, we had parents who could barely speak English. A lot of times, we'd be almost ashamed of them because of that. That seems like an awful thing to say now, but that's what we felt when we were kids. Sometimes the other kids would exclude us from things just because we were Italian.

"We developed an attitude back then of, 'It's us Italians against the rest of the world.' I think Babe has always shown that. That's not the way it is now for Italian kids, thank God, but we all felt it back then."

But Joe LaCava, now retired after teaching Italian for twenty-five years at Drake University in Des Moines and also a keen Babe watcher, disputes that.

"I'm not sure that the Italianness is that big a thing in his life," LaCava said. "Despite the fact that he runs Italian restaurants, and despite that much of the outside world thinks of him when they think of Italians, I don't see that great, intense Italian pride in him.

"You can talk about how he's irascible one moment and then a big pussycat the next, but those really aren't ethnic characteristics. That's just Babe."

*B*abe Bisignano's fame knows few bounds in Iowa or nationally. When he played "Big Jule" in a Des Moines Community Playhouse production of Guys and Dolls, the playhouse not only packed the place, it had to extend the run of the play. Shriners have made him an honorary member. He's visited popes and presidents and governors. But he counts as one of his proudest moments the time when Dubuque Wahlert Catholic High School officials, mindful of the fact that he had had only an eighth-grade education, granted him an honorary high school diploma. His celebrity is such that, even on occasions when he's been hospitalized, he can't be far from the phone, which is always ringing.

In Guys and Dolls.

Babe, the Shriner.

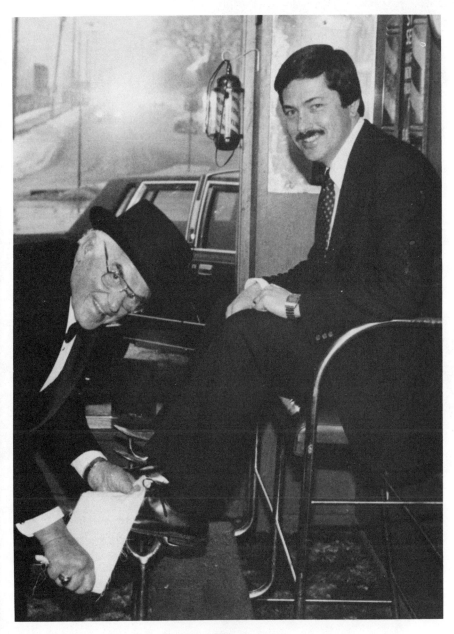

Shining Governor Branstad's shoes.

Meeting Pope John XXIII.

Meeting President Carter.

Meeting presidential candidate Alexander Haig.

The Graduate.

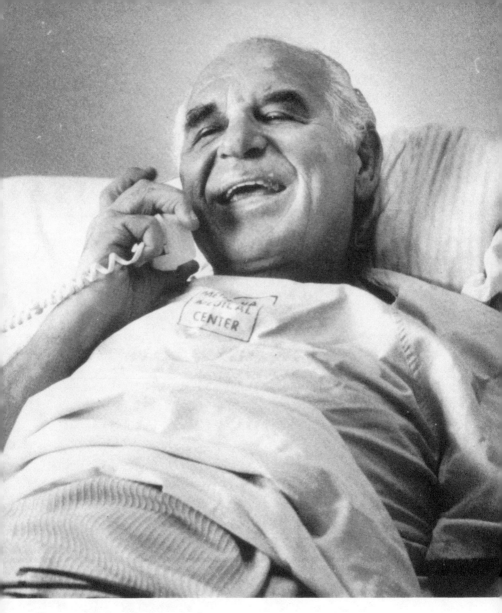

Busy even in the hospital.

14

THE FUTURE

"...if Mary Magdalene...could make it to heaven, then I can, too."

HE CAN BE SUCH A ... such a ... what word do I really want to use here? I guess it would be the one that's come up so embarrassingly often in this book: such a son of a bitch.

I've seen Babe Bisignano unleash it on employees. I've seen him unleash it on friends. His kids have told me how he's unleashed it on them. And now he's unleashed it on me.

So why do I still admire him? Why can I honestly say I still like him?

"If he perceives you as his friend, there's nothing he won't do for you," said Fred Eckrosh, who knows him so well. "If he perceives you as his enemy, he won't speak to you."

Al Couppee has an interesting perspective on that. Couppee, sixty-eight and retired in Canyon Lake, California, is a longtime Bisignano friend who came out of Council Bluffs decades ago to become the quarterback on the famed "Ironmen" football team at the University of Iowa in 1939. That's when he first met Babe. They even wrestled together once at the YMCA in Des Moines. Couppee then worked as sports anchor for KRNT-TV, now KCCI-TV, in Des Moines for thirteen years before bolting for California and big-time broadcasting success in professional football. But he retains his friendship with Babe.

"With Babe," he said, "it's either feast or famine. Among the people who've met him, they either love him or they hate him, which is the way it is for most all of us who have strong feelings and express them. It's more so that way for Babe because he's also always been so ready to back up what he says with whatever it takes. I've known the guy a long, long time, and I'm well aware of all his faults. But I also know his virtues, and there are a lot of them. That's why I stand by him. I'm one of those that in my eyes, he can do no wrong."

Does Babe have dreams? Does he look ahead and imagine a better life here? He certainly imagines a better life hereafter. "I keep telling myself," he said, "that if Mary Magdalene, who was a prostitute, could make it to heaven, then I can, too."

But what about here? Will it get better? Can it? This came up in an interview I conducted with him early on a Saturday morning at his home. The interview was interrupted repeatedly by phone calls, all having to do with the fact that some young pizza maker had said she was not going to make it to work downtown that day and so Babe was facing the possibility he might have to operate without one, find another one, or do it himself—and he doesn't know how to make a pizza.

The calls went back and forth to other employees, to other restaurant owners. This seventy-five-year-old mega-success was practically begging for a one-day pizza maker.

Does he have dreams? "I dream that there'll come a day when I can wake up in the morning and realize that I don't have one damned thing to worry about and don't really have one damned thing to do that day," he said. "If the telephone rings, it will be someone saying hello instead of someone saying they can't be at work.

"I'm convinced I'm going to die with my boots on at the restaurant some night, but I want you to pray for me that I can sell the downtown place. Then I could take my good people up to the little joint up north, and we could do it so easy. I wouldn't have to be there all the time.

"I'd have time to travel. I'd take half of the money I got from selling downtown and I'd give it away. I'd take the other half and go to Italy and show them what a Big Man I am. It's fun to think of me in Italy, isn't it?"

It is.

But he wouldn't spend all his time in Italy, or at his new little restaurant on the north side of Des Moines. "No," he said. "I'll tell you what I'd really like to be able to do. Dubuque is a special place for me, you know. I've got my little daughter buried up there. And remember when Dubuque Wahlert High School gave me an honorary high school diploma because I'd never had one? I'd like to get to where I could go spend a lot of time up there.

"I'd want to find some place there where I could do some work. What I want is to have a place where I could get some overalls—I haven't had a pair since I was a kid—and I could go out and trim some grass and take orders and do whatever needed to be done for a few hours every day. Then I'd be off and I'd have my golf clubs and I'd go play a little golf. Then I'd have a few beers with my friends and then I'd go to bed. And there'd be no phone ringing when I woke up the next morning."

Of course, anybody with any financial sense at all knows that Babe Bisignano could do that today. He could buy half of Dubuque if he wanted to. So why doesn't he?

What comes to mind is something his wife Katy would tell him whenever he'd screwed up, fallen short, or made a fool of himself. "She'd always say, 'You can't make a race-horse out of a mule,' " he said, and then he laughed about how accurate that really is in his case. At least he recognizes it.

And doesn't that bring back that line about how his kids refer to him today as "Our Founder, The Mule"?

The Mule works.

The Mule is stubborn.

The Mule wants life to be lived on his terms.

Who doesn't?

CHUCK OFFENBURGER, one of Iowa's most popular journalists, writes the "Iowa Boy" column for the *Des Moines Register*. Offenburger has won more than thirty-five journalism awards during his career, including induction into the national leadership honorary Omicron Delta Kappa by officials of Drake University, who cited him "for his interest in, and compassion for, the people of Iowa." In 1983 he received a special citation from Wartburg College in Waverly for "his unerring eye for capturing the human drama that makes Iowa uniquely Iowa." Besides writing the column, Offenburger is co-leader, with John Karras, of RAGBRAI—the *Register*'s Annual Great Bicycle Ride Across Iowa. He is also the author of *Iowa Boy: Ten Years of Columns by Chuck Offenburger*, published by Iowa State University Press in 1987.

163